KIRK
CAMERON
DREAM
GUY

KIRK CAMERON

DREAM GUY

GRACE
CATALANO

BANTAM BOOKS
TORONTO · NEW YORK · LONDON · SYDNEY · AUCKLAND

KIRK CAMERON: DREAM GUY

A Bantam Book / November 1987

*The Starfire logo is a registered trademark of Bantam Books, Inc.
Registered in U.S. Patent and Trademark Office and elsewhere*

*Produced by Connie Berman and Roseann Hirsch of
Ultra Communications Inc.*

ISBN 0-553-27135-0

Published simultaneously in the United States and Canada

PRINTED IN THE UNITED STATES OF AMERICA

O   0 9 8 7 6 5 4 3 2

For Mom, Dad, and Joseph
And for Connie and Roseann

CONTENTS

INTRODUCTION 1
1. A PROMISING START 7
2. AFTER-SCHOOL ACTING 24
3. SCORING A TOUCHDOWN 35
4. INSTANT STARDOM 41
5. TOP TEENAGE HEARTTHROB 58
6. THE GROWING PAINS FAMILY 66
7. LIFE OFF SCREEN 71
8. THE GIRL FOR KIRK 81
9. LIKE FATHER, LIKE SON 85
10. LOOKING AHEAD 90
KIRK'S VITAL STATISTICS 95
KIRK TRIVIA 97
KIRK'S WORDS OF WISDOM 100

INTRODUCTION

"**Q**uiet in the studio!"

The voice silences an eager crowd waiting to see the taping of their favorite television show and the appearance of their favorite young actor.

As the soundstage darkens, light streams across a familiar set; the living room of the Seavers' house. The cameras begin to roll as a slim, curly-haired young man bursts through the front door. With a confident grin and a twinkle in his eye, Kirk Cameron is in motion and the popular TV show *Growing Pains*, captures the attention of millions of viewers. Though he's been acting only a few short years, it's easy to see how comfortable Kirk is before the cameras. His timing is perfect, and the natural ability he projects brings a refreshing air to the wisecracking character he portrays so perfectly each week.

As the show ends, the cast members make their bows to the studio audience, which has just witnessed a piece of television history. Almost in unison, the screams shriek the name, "Kirk! Kirk! Kirk!" A smile breaks out on Kirk Cameron's face, and he puts up his hand and waves to the crowd of teenage girls.

Kirk Cameron. The top teen heartthrob in the country today. But there is much more to this young man than that designation suggests.

Only a few years ago no one had heard of Kirk Cameron. Yet in less than one year he managed to draw in fans by the thousands, fans attracted by his twinkling hazel eyes, baby-smooth skin, and the overall contour and configuration of his perfectly shaped, flawless face.

Many teen idols have come and gone over the years. Though some captured attention and won female hearts, none have caused the sensation that Kirk is causing. He is reminiscent of the kind of teen idols of the past, such as Elvis Presley, Bobby Sherman, David Cassidy, and Shaun Cassidy, who burst quickly onto the teen scene and then dominated the covers of every major teen magazine. Kirk is the first teen idol in a long time to bring excitement back to teenage girls everywhere.

Unlike recent teen idols Rob Lowe, Ralph Macchio, and Michael J. Fox, Kirk is different. He's younger, and he really enjoys his teen-idol status, admitting, "My mom saves everything that's written about me!"

Kirk Cameron, with his appealing personality and winning smile, really is like the boy next door, and it was these qualities that were immediately recognized by Michael Sullivan, executive producer of *Growing Pains.* When casting started, Sullivan was looking for an eighteen-year-old actor to play Mike Seaver, but the innocence that Kirk brought to the character during his audition convinced the producer that he was perfect for the role.

Kirk's irresistible charm is part of the reason why millions of girls everywhere dream of him as their ideal guy. He is unspoiled and unaffected by the trappings of Hollywood, and because he has remained well adjusted and levelheaded about his skyrocketing career, he is an inspiration to the girls who adore him.

The proof of this comes in the form of over ten thousand letters a month that are delivered to him at the offices of both ABC and Warner Brothers Television. Some fans want to meet him in person, while others just write him a letter to express how much they love him and the show. And then, of course, there are thousands of requests for autographed photos. All this attention is certainly flattering to this once shy and withdrawn boy. "When I'm asked for my autograph, I can't say no," he admits with a shy grin. "I think meeting a lot of people is part of the fun of being an actor."

With his good looks and easygoing personality, Kirk is now at the height of his profession. He is making the transition from television to movies as his popularity continues to grow by leaps and bounds. At seventeen, Kirk has a spotlight shining on him that will get brighter with time. He has many choices open to him, and any road he decides to take will surely lead him to greater stardom.

Though it may appear as if Kirk Cameron was an overnight sensation, the climb up the ladder of success is never easy, even when it seems quick and trouble-free. As a child actor in over thirty television commercials, Kirk spent his early years traveling after school with his mother, Barbara, from one audition to the next. The young, ambitious actor soon won many acting jobs, devoting himself entirely to his career. Many child actors crumble under the pressures of school and work, but not Kirk. He has the drive and strength needed to pursue acting and is able to juggle his career and schoolwork with ease.

Though he had always dreamed of going into medicine, Kirk now feels acting is his chosen profession. "I'm still planning on going to college after I graduate from high school," he explains. "But right now I'm really interested in acting. I want to take that as far as I can, and see what happens."

Success can change a person drastically, but Kirk makes it known that nothing has changed for him, either at home or at school. His home life remains like any normal teenager's. He is still expected to help with household chores, which he does without a qualm. And he doesn't mind keeping his bedroom neat and clean—he describes himself as a "neat freak" who has to have everything in order.

His soaring success hasn't interrupted what he truly believes in. Two years ago this health-conscious young man started following the Pritikin diet, and he is very strict about staying on it.

There aren't many teen idols who take such things so seriously, but Kirk Cameron is the kind of guy who does everything with perfection. After all, in only one year he has captured almost the entire teen and preteen TV audience.

When *Growing Pains* made its TV debut, Kirk became a hero almost overnight, reaching super-stardom, which will, no doubt, lead him to greater heights. He has many dreams and many years in which to fulfill them, and it's exciting to think that his fans will be with him every step of the way!

1. *A PROMISING START*

Kirk Thomas Cameron was born on October 12, 1970, in Panorama City, California, to Robert and Barbara Cameron. His father, a physical education teacher at a local junior high school, and his mother, an entrepreneur of her own cookie business called Chocolate Chip Lace, were barely out of their teens when they met, married, and started raising a family.

What especially attracted eighteen-year-old Barbara to tall, dark, and handsome Robert was his charm and smile. Like his son, Kirk, Robert always had a terrific sense of humor, and Barbara loved spending hours with him, laughing and talking. They dated for less than a year before they decided to get married.

Their special day took place in the year 1969; a troubled, as well as triumphant, time for the world. While the Vietnamese War raged on with no relief in sight, television audiences were witnessing film of the first man to set foot on the moon and astronauts Neil A. Armstrong, Edwin E. Aldrin, Jr., and Michael Collins became America's heroes.

Star Trek, which would go into syndication and

become one of the biggest hits of all time, was canceled in 1969. The show had been taken off the air the year before due to sagging ratings. But fans had picketed Paramount and written thousands of letters to keep the show on the air, and it had been renewed for one more season.

One of *Star Trek*'s biggest fans was Robert Cameron, who watched the show faithfully every Friday night at 8:30 P.M. He especially liked the character Captain Kirk and had decided early on that when he had a son, he would be named Kirk.

The Camerons were so happy in their first year of marriage that the outside world and its troubles didn't affect them at all. They were only married a few months when the news came that they were going to become parents, and Robert and Barbara talked endlessly about having a boy.

Somehow Barbara knew she'd have more children later and wanted her firstborn to be the big brother other children could lean on. Barbara was very close to her mother, Jeanne, and her sister, Carol, and she spent most of 1970 getting ready for the birth of her first child: buying toys and clothes and fixing up a small room in the apartment she shared with her husband.

Finally, in mid-October, Barbara gave birth to a beautiful, healthy baby boy. She said her blond-haired, blue/green-eyed baby was "the most beautiful boy I had ever seen" and that his birth was the product of the strong love she and Robert shared. Barbara chose Thomas for her son's middle name after her father, Frank Thomas, and the Camerons settled in a comfortable California suburb.

As a baby, Kirk used to love to sit by himself and play quietly. The ever-smiling Kirk was a good baby who was shy but loved attention. Because he was Robert and Barbara's firstborn, attention was one thing he got plenty of. Both his parents and grandparents loved picking him up, holding him, and talking to him. Kirk was a very responsive and lovable baby who rarely frowned and made everyone around him feel happy.

Before he was a year old, Kirk went on his first family vacation with his mother and father. Robert's twin sister had asked the Camerons to visit her at her home in Switzerland because she was anxious to see her new little nephew. Robert wanted to spend time with his sister and felt it would be the perfect trip for his family. Barbara was already seven months pregnant with their second child, so it was the only time they went on vacation as a family of three.

They spent a very enjoyable five weeks in Switzerland, and before they came home, Kirk had already taken his first steps. Dressed in a one-piece jumpsuit with short pants, baby Kirk was determined to begin walking. Robert and Barbara had nicknamed their bundle of joy "Boo Boo," and when he was learning to walk, they'd enthusiastically cheer him on with outstretched arms. "Come on, Boo Boo!" Determined, Kirk would walk excitedly toward his parents, and Barbara says with pride, "By the time we left Switzerland, he was really moving around."

When Kirk was eleven months old, Barbara gave birth to another baby, a girl she named Bridgette.

Though Kirk was still very young, his mother prepared him for the new baby, and when Bridgette was born, Kirk was thrilled. He welcomed his new baby sister with open arms, and with only an eleven-month age difference between them, they grew very close to each other.

Barbara made sure she devoted an equal amount of love and attention to both her children. It was evident right from the beginning that sibling rivalry was the farthest thing from Kirk's and Bridgette's young minds. "They were so adorable together," says Barbara. "I almost felt like I had twins."

On October 12, 1971, Kirk celebrated his first birthday. His parents bought him a small cake and threw him a party in his grandmother's house in Northridge, California. The bright-eyed, perky one-year-old was given a xylophone by his parents, which gave him his first taste of making his own music. Kirk would bang on his xylophone for hours, impressed by the different sounds that came out of it. As he grew older, music remained a field that continued to interest him.

When Kirk was four years old and his sister, Bridgette, was three, Barbara decided to go back to college and take some courses. "I was lucky," she says. "Right next to the college there was a preschool where I could leave the kids."

Kirk and Bridgette enjoyed preschool but never let each other out of one another's sight. Both of the Cameron kids were shy, and it took them time to make new friends. But when they did, the friendships were strong. Even now, with all his popularity, Kirk remains friendly with people he's known for a long time. He is the kind of guy who makes a friend for life, and he confides, "I only have one or two really good friends. They're people I grew up with and know that I can really count on when I need them."

Kirk was a very impressionable child whose early interests in sports and music developed more and more as he grew older. "I was just about four years old when I got my first bike," exults Kirk. "It was a Schwinn and I loved it!"

By the time he entered kindergarten, the Camerons had moved from the San Fernando Valley to a house in Fillmore, California, a beautiful suburb north of Los Angeles. Kirk liked school and was a good student. He was always the kind of kid who did everything that was expected of him, and even though he liked sports, he devoted most of his time to schoolwork.

At the age of five, Kirk was settled into his new environment, but because he was shy, he kept to himself. He had made some friends in his new neighborhood, but most of the kids he went to school with didn't live near his home. In 1975, the Camerons welcomed another baby into their household as Barbara gave birth to Melissa, a beautiful, brown-haired girl. Kirk and Bridgette now had a new playmate, and as the children grew older, they grew closer.

Just as Barbara had hoped for, Kirk was the big brother his younger sisters could lean on. A fourth child, Candace, was born the following year, and Kirk was, and is, always there for his sisters. As a young boy, when he became interested in girls, he liked the fact that he could ask his sisters for advice whenever he had a question about the opposite sex. Now that his sisters are getting older, they ask Kirk questions about boys.

"I feel good when one of my sisters comes to me and wants my advice," he says, "because it shows that they trust me enough to ask. I think the four of us have a real good relationship."

Young Kirk's creativity and talents began showing up in many areas as a young boy. His early interest in music never left him, and every time he went to visit his grandmother, he would lift up the cover of her piano and bang on the keys.

"I was really interested in learning to play," he remembers. "My grandmother had this real old piano that she played all the time, and she was really good. So I asked her if she would teach me." Kirk's grandmother began giving her eager-to-learn grandson piano lessons, and he was beginning to pick it up very quickly. He learned all the scales and went through the beginner's music book in a matter of a few months. But like many young boys his age, he discovered soccer and skateboarding and gave up his passion for the piano.

By joining the school soccer team, Kirk made all new friends, a few of whom he became very close to. When his school day was almost over, Kirk would begin to grow impatient waiting for the final bell to ring.

The practice field was right behind his school, and every day at three he would be out there with the team, practicing and working out. Soccer became Kirk's new passion and ultimately began to bring him out of his shyness. He was very athletic, and it seemed that he was able to master everything he tried.

One Saturday his friends had acquired a skateboard they were trying to balance on. Skateboarding had become America's newest trend, and when it was at its peak, there were an estimated twenty-five million skateboarders in America. Young Kirk wanted to be one of those millions and decided to spend his time learning how to master the sport. But he tried to learn too fast, and one day, to his chagrin, he lost his balance and fell off.

Landing on one hand, he got right up but was in a considerable amount of pain. He held his hand very tightly, but the pain didn't stop, and he ran into his house crying. When Barbara looked at her son's limp hand, she knew immediately it was broken. She hugged Kirk to try to calm him down.

"Kirk, honey, stop crying. I'm going to take you to the doctor so he can look at your hand. Okay?"

Kirk wiped his tears and nodded. He climbed into the backseat of the family car, and his mother began driving to the hospital. Barbara noticed how quiet he was and kept checking him through the mirror to see if he was all right.

He was just sitting very still, sobbing. "Are you okay, Kirk?" his mother asked with concern.

He looked up, his expressive hazel eyes filled with sadness and asked, "Mommy, am I going to die?"

Barbara stopped the car and turned to face her son. "No," she told him gently, suddenly realizing that this was the first time he had experienced any

13

kind of real pain and just didn't understand what was happening.

When Barbara thinks back to that day now, she says, "My heart was breaking for him because he was so young and so frightened."

Though Kirk wore a cast until his hand healed, he was right back playing soccer and learning to master that skateboard. Once young Kirk was turned on to sports, he wanted to try everything.

"It was my dad who influenced me to care about my health at such an early age," he asserts. "He's an incredible athlete, and as I got older he'd take me with him to the gym so we could work out together. In the summer I usually go out with my dad at six-thirty in the morning. We play racquetball, then head to the gym for a good workout and weight lifting, and then go to the beach in Santa Monica. The beach is my favorite place, and Santa Monica is where Dad used to spend his time as a kid, so it's really fun."

The one thing the Camerons really put a family effort into is their yearly vacation together. With four kids in the family, Robert bought a trailer for vacations, and their summers were spent traveling to Lake Millerton for camping trips. Somehow the fact that Kirk was able to get close to nature has always appealed to him. Now, more than ever, he looks forward to time off so he can relax with his family and get away from the city, and the work. Vacations with his family have always been very important to Kirk, and he treasures every minute spent with his parents and sisters.

"Once we drove to Dixon, Illinois, to visit my

aunt," he recalls. "That trip was great. We were away for nine days, and on the way we stopped off at Mount Rushmore and it was very impressive!"

By the time Kirk was nine years old, he was just like any other boy his age. He went to school, played all kinds of sports, spent time with close friends, listened to his favorite music on the stereo, and went to the beach. Acting never entered Kirk's mind, nor did it enter the minds of his parents or sisters.

Robert and Barbara hadn't planned on acting careers for Kirk and his three sisters, but in less than one year they all would plunge into the entertainment world. There were no performers on either side of Robert's or Barbara's families, so they didn't know anything about breaking into show business. But the advice of a very persistent and helpful neighbor changed all that.

Francine Rich is the mother of Adam Rich, who played Nicholas Bradford on television's smash-hit family drama, *Eight Is Enough*. The show, which premiered on ABC as a replacement in March 1977, was a sixty-minute comedy-drama starring Dick Van Patten and the late Diana Hyland as the parents of eight children. The day-to-day events that shaped the lives of this Sacramento, California, family was basically the premise of each show, and it was an instant hit.

As the youngest member of the Bradford family, Adam Rich was a charmer who added wit to each show and became very well known to television audiences. Living next door to Kirk, he struck up a good friendship with him that they still share today.

What was especially interesting to them is the fact that—although Adam is two years older—both he and Kirk were born on the same day—October 12. Subsequently they shared many of the same interests and hobbies, and when Adam wasn't filming his TV show or going to school, he enjoyed spending time at Kirk's house and playing sports with him.

At the same time Adam's mom, Fran, had become a very good friend of Barbara Cameron, and when she wasn't with Adam on the set, she would spend hours conversing with her next-door neighbor. While the two women would be having a leisurely afternoon talk, Kirk and his sisters would dash by. Whether the girls were coming home from school or Kirk was running out to play soccer, Fran watched them and knew they were perfect for the cameras.

One day she said to Barbara, "Why don't you try to do something with your kids? They're so adorable." But Barbara shrugged the idea off. Somehow it didn't seem possible that they could break into show business just like that, so she didn't give it a second thought.

When Barbara showed Fran pictures of her sister's wedding, which the Cameron family had attended in 1979, she flipped to the snapshot of the four kids. Bridgette, Melissa, and Candace were flower girls and wore matching dresses, and Kirk was all decked out in a tuxedo, complete with ruffled shirt and bow tie.

Fran held the snapshot up and said, "You really

should get an agent and get your kids into commercials."

Barbara hesitated again, but Fran's perseverance continued. Clutching the photo, she said, "You know what I'm going to do? I'm going to send this photo of the kids to Adam's agent. Can I borrow it?"

Barbara smiled and responded with an uncertain, "Go ahead."

Kirk and the girls didn't know at that time that their mother had even sent their photo out to an agent, and she decided she wouldn't say a word. Both she and Robert figured nothing would come of it and didn't want their kids to get their hopes up high for something Barbara felt could never happen.

For a few days nothing further was spoken of the matter, until one afternoon when the telephone rang. Barbara answered it in her usual cheerful manner. It was the agent's office, and they were calling to say they were interested in the kids. "We'd like to set up a time to meet them," the voice said.

A feeling of disbelief fell over Barbara, and at first she wasn't sure what she wanted to do. It had happened so quickly that she needed to think the whole thing through before she took her children in to meet with an agent. Of course, the thought of her children being on television excited her, but she knew it would be hard work, and they were still so young for such responsibilities.

She decided to congregate the family into the living room after supper and ask if the children were interested in entering show business.

"How would you feel about going on television?" Barbara asked, and watched the four young faces light up. Sensing their sudden excitement, she warned, "First we have to meet an agent and see what happens, and then you'll have to audition."

But all four children were interested and understood that acting would take a great amount of work. On the day they were to meet the agent they went to school as usual. The meeting was set for late afternoon, and when Barbara picked up her children, she made sure they looked their absolute best.

The family trooped into the agent's office in a line with Kirk at the back. The most outgoing of the children was Bridgette, whom Barbara figured would be the most likely candidate for an acting career. As it turned out, the agent liked all four children and signed them up, with Kirk being singled out as the one with the most potential.

He sat quietly in the office and spoke in a whisper, still unsure of what this was all about. At that point Barbara thought Kirk didn't have a chance, but when he smiled, his face lit up the whole room and the agent remarked to Barbara, "I want to try him for one year. He has the right look. I think I can get him work."

Kirk nervously stared in disbelief at his mother, and the news set him afire with excitement. Now that he was being represented by an agent and saw that someone else believed he could succeed in the business, he decided he was really going to give acting his best shot.

"I've always lived by one rule," Kirk explains sincerely. "I don't like to do something or not do something just because someone else says it's good or bad."

The decision for Kirk to enter show business brought out his natural abilities to act, and acting showed him what he was born to do. He hadn't taken any formal lessons but picked up on acting very quickly. From the time he stepped onto the soundstage of his first job as an actor, he knew it was something he wanted to keep working at and to improve.

"I really like to act," he confides today. "I went into it and stuck with it because I really do enjoy it, not because I was hoping to become a famous star."

At the very start it almost looked as if maybe his mother, Fran Rich, and his agent might have been setting too many goals for him. The first interview he went on was for a Coca-Cola commercial, and to everyone's disappointment he didn't get the job. Everyone seemed so positive that Kirk would conquer the television world in no time. After all, at nine, he was an adorable boy with a captivating smile, sandy blond hair, and big blue-green eyes.

Unfortunately the unknown child actor would start to learn the rejection many have to go through in show business. Deep down inside, Kirk really didn't expect to win the first commercial he auditioned for. Even at a young age he was realistic, and with the love, guidance, and support of his parents he was able to handle all the pressures he found himself under.

The hope that Kirk was Hollywood's bright new star never diminished in the mind of his agent, and she set up as many commercial auditions as she could for him. Almost every day the young hopeful would climb into his mother's car, and together they would drive to interviews and tryouts. Because of this, Kirk found he had to give up some things, such as sports, music, and most after-school activities. He didn't even have time to ride his bicycle up and down the street in front of his home anymore.

Sometimes Kirk felt like giving up the grind of the acting business. He would sit in waiting rooms and think of going home to rest and study for school.

"I remember seeing the same group of kids every day," he recalls. "We were all competing for the same jobs."

The second and third interviews proved unsuccessful for Kirk, and at this very vulnerable age it made him realize how much harder he had to work at achieving his goal. "I honestly believe that there is more rejection in acting than in any other field," Kirk confesses. The early auditions became rigorous for him, and he admits that if his mother hadn't been there to guide him through the heartbreak, he never would have had the patience to continue his climb up the ladder of success.

"I owe it all to my mom," he says with a smile. "It really would have been impossible without her support. I'm glad things started to work out with my career because my mom really likes the fact that I'm in show business."

On the days Barbara wasn't taking Kirk on auditions, she would pick up one of her girls and drive her to the many commercial interviews in town.

As far back as when television first began, early advertisers and producers of television commercials figured out that the sweet face of a child helped to sell their products. Whether it was for cereal, toys, or cleansers, children somehow added to the appeal of the product being sold.

The setting of the American family and their daily use of a product is probably one reason why kids in commercials become so popular. But other reasons are that kids like to see other kids on TV, and adults take notice when a child is especially wholesome and innocent.

Candace Cameron projected these qualities even under the age of four. She was a perky, pudgy-cheeked little girl who was as cute as a button and charmed all the casting people and directors she met. When the right part came along, little Candace was called and was the first Cameron to appear on television.

From her first commercial, doors were opened for Kirk's youngest sister, and she began appearing in one commercial after another, everything from McDonald's to Cabbage Patch Kids dolls. Her early exposure to acting was a strong one, and she is the only Cameron girl who wants to continue working in the business.

Though Candace was the first celebrity in the Cameron household, it didn't take long for Kirk to catch the attention of producers and begin his own career. While helping Candace go over scripts, he began to really like acting and worked hard at improving his craft.

While most youngsters Kirk's age start with enthusiasm to do something creative, many soon tire. But Kirk didn't. His desire and determination to learn the techniques of acting continued and deepened, and he was more compelled than ever to succeed. Although acting was fun, Kirk knew it was work and was prepared to put his all into it.

The call came early in the morning. Barbara was to take Kirk on another commercial audition after school for Super Sugar Crisp cereal. It was the sixth interview he would be going on, and he had decided to smile more, speak louder, and make a better and more lasting impression.

The audition would be held in the late afternoon, and Kirk spent his day in school watching the time, waiting for three o'clock. Although he didn't falter in any of his classes, he had a strong feeling about this particular interview and couldn't wait to get to the audition.

As always, the large waiting room was filled with young hopefuls and their mothers, all wanting this to be their lucky break. Anxiety built up inside Kirk, and when his name was called, he and Barbara walked into the room where the auditions were being held.

Since he had been studying scripts with his sister, cold reading now came more easily to him. But he recalls today, "I was very nervous. I cried throughout the whole thing."

In spite of his tears, his acting caught the attention of the director and even surprised Barbara. For the first time she really felt as if Kirk had done a good job.

Now that it was over, only time would tell if the

agency's client also thought Kirk was good. He and his mother tried to forget about it, but Kirk was anxiously awaiting the answer. Every time the phone rang, he was hoping to hear something about the audition. Even if it was another rejection, at least he would learn the outcome and realize he had to work even harder for the next audition. While he tried to find a way to calm his nerves and stop the butterflies he felt in his stomach during auditions, the phone finally rang.

This time the answer was yes, and Kirk Cameron was signed for his very first television commercial for Super Sugar Crisp cereal. With the anticipation finally over, Kirk was now ready to embark on the acting career that ultimately would lead him to the top.

2. *AFTER-SCHOOL ACTING*

Kirk Cameron's first opportunity for real performing would be to taste Super Sugar Crisp cereal and exclaim how much he liked it. It seemed like a cinch, and Kirk thought he would go to the studio, read the few lines he had memorized, eat a little cereal, and leave.

He later realized that commericals were time-consuming and it took many many hours until the director was absolutely satisfied. Because so many takes of one scene were filmed, Kirk not only would have to act out his same few lines a number of times, but also he was expected to eat the cereal during every take. It was a job the young actor didn't mind accepting at the beginning of his career. But as Kirk grew older, he began caring more about his health and about the types and amounts of food he ate.

"Sometimes you can't keep eating the same thing over and over," he quips, remembering the long days of filming in the studio. "There were times I just didn't like it."

When his first television commercial was finished and ready to air, the entire Cameron family sat around the set waiting to see Kirk on TV. Robert

24

and Barbara were very proud and excited when they first saw their two little actors on television.

Studying his every move on screen, Kirk saw a few things in the commercial that he thought he could have done differently. He is always very critical of himself, trying to correct any flaw he notices in his performance. While he knew he would do better the next time, his first commercial was a success and secured his name in Hollywood. Kirk's natural ability and good looks were immediately recognized by producers, and there was soon a demand for him.

With the year 1980 approaching, Kirk found himself in the middle of a very productive time in his career. By the end of the year, he had appeared in over thirty commercials for products such as soft drinks, cheese, Polaroid cameras, toys, and cereal.

He would go to school in the morning for about three hours, then Barbara would pick him up at noon and drive him to a studio where he would work on the new commercials he was filming. Fortunately Kirk's school agreed to allow Kirk a special schedule.

As for Kirk, he pushed himself to be the best he could be in both areas because he cared about his work and about his grades. Learning to adjust to his career as an actor and fulfill his responsibilities as a student isn't always easy, he admits. "It's complicated sometimes, but I've been able to get used to it. Luckily most of my teachers cooperated with my busy schedule, and that made it a little easier."

Kirk was a good student who worked steadily at improving his acting every day. At the age of eleven he began to break away from commercials because he was auditioning for roles on TV. Being a preteen actor, the parts he won were often supporting roles. Though these parts would lead Kirk to the success he is enjoying today, there was no way he could possibly have foreseen his future then. He continued, however, to strive toward his ultimate goal.

Kirk's first parts were small guest-starring roles on the TV shows *Bret Maverick*, *Lou Grant*, and *Code Red*. Walking onto the set of a television show he watched every week was certainly a thrill for Kirk. He marveled at the way the shows were filmed and was very interested in learning every detail of how television programs were made.

Though the sets of a TV show looked the same as the commercial sets, Kirk realized that television required hard work to achieve a great performance. Even though he was just guest-starring in small roles, he spent long hours on the set studying the cameras and props.

In the beginning he had a difficult time adjusting to the routine of following the white pieces of tape on the floor (called marks). They are usually placed in designated spots to guide an actor around the stage so it appears as if he is moving casually.

Different from the filming of commercials where the scene usually takes place in one setting, the staging of a television show must take care as to where each actor will stand. The casual movements of the actor as he reads his lines must appear natural.

Kirk had been used to sitting at a kitchen table for the shooting of cereal or soda commercials.

When he arrived on the set of his first television show, the director sat down with him and explained the importance of staying on his mark.

"If you move one step too far or too short, you're out of camera range," the director explained. "If that happens, we have to reshoot the entire scene."

Though Kirk understood how crucial his actions were to the filming of a scene, he still found it hard to balance himself on the mark near a specific corner of the room. He can't remember how many times in the beginning the director shouted, "Kirk, you missed the mark!"

Though their job is tedious and often mind-boggling, directors were always patient with Kirk because they could see that he had an enormous amount of potential as an actor. One director said of him, "He wanted to learn everything. You could see in his eyes how much the filming interested him."

Kirk soon mastered the technique of staying on his marks. There wasn't anything he couldn't do once he set his mind to it. Even though shooting a television show consisted of long hours of standing still for costume fittings and speaking at different octaves so his voice could be tested and adjusted for sound levels, Kirk listened to everything carefully and followed all instructions.

His innocence and early excitement for the business are two qualities he still possesses. He remains as humble as the first day he entered show business and says, "I guess I'll always be the same, because that's me. My family knows to tell me if I ever start to act differently. If I begin to act like Mr. Show Business, I want to know before it gets out of hand. That way I'll be able to stop it."

Kirk is very serious about remaining unspoiled, even though he is the top teen idol today. "Success may change a few things," he confides, "but I learned early in my career that I can't let it change who I am. Sure, I spend my time a little differently, but I'm still the same Kirk I was before I became well known."

At just twelve years old he plunged into a television career he hadn't planned. The young, bright-eyed actor was gaining a good reputation in Hollywood as a hard worker, and producers and directors were impressed with his talent.

By the time Kirk was thirteen, he had been working steadily at acting for over two years and was eager to continue. From his three small guest appearances on television shows, Kirk was up for many television movies and after-school specials. He was now easily recognized; his résumé held a long and impressive list of credits.

In one year Kirk appeared in three TV movies, *Goliath Awaits*, *Children of the Crossfire*, and *Starflight One*. The roles he won were usually as the child of the lead character, but Kirk was now hoping to land bigger and more interesting parts.

An early Disney TV movie entitled *Beyond Witch Mountain* provided him with a better role and introduced him to Tracey Gold. She was the star of the movie, and the two young stars liked each other right from the beginning. Though they didn't know it at the time, Tracey would appear with Kirk again in *The Best of Times* and on *Growing Pains*, and become the only actress to strike up a lasting friendship with him and his sisters.

When Kirk entered Lawrence Junior High School, he was the school's celebrity. He always tried to keep a low profile about his acting career, but there was no getting around the success he had achieved in such a short time.

The girls in school especially took notice of Kirk and liked him. He was shy, and before his popularity in the entertainment world, he hadn't really gotten to know too many of his classmates. Now there were some who really wanted to get to know him. He liked a few girls but was too bashful to ask anyone out.

"I was always very shy around girls, especially if I liked them," he divulges hesitantly. When he entered the ninth grade, he caught the eye of a girl he wanted to ask out. She would casually say something to Kirk every day, but he would blush and walk away.

Finally he decided to ask her out. She said yes, and Kirk's first date consisted of going to the movies after supper on a Friday night. They went out a few more times after that, but Kirk's work on television took him away from the school for many months out of the year. His friendship with his first girlfriend unfortunately came to an end.

In 1983, he auditioned for and won the role of Eric Armstrong for a new show called *Two Marriages*. The show was in the tradition of hour-long family dramas such as *Family* and *Eight Is Enough* and was centered around the lives of two families who lived next door to each other.

Basically the show was drama, but comedy managed to seep through once in a while. Like all sixty-minute family shows at that time, all cast members got their chance at having an episode revolve around them. It was Kirk's opportunity to prove his comedic and dramatic acting abilities, and he was able to play both with ease.

When he was asked what he preferred to do, he said honestly, "Drama is more of a challenge to me than comedy. But I like comedy better because I like to laugh and have fun with a character. If I have to, I can get emotional in dramatic scenes, but I'd rather tell a few jokes."

The producers of *Two Marriages* thought Kirk and C. Thomas Howell, a popular teen idol, would draw in a young audience and make it a monumental success. But, unfortunately, it was canceled after just one season on the air.

Kirk had enjoyed working on his first television series and had hoped it would last longer than it did. It was a good first experience for him and prepared him for future television jobs. It also gave him the first real disappointment he had known. The sudden cancellation of *Two Marriages* after only one brief season devastated the young actor.

"I was sorry to see it end because I really had a good time working on that show," Kirk commented later. "It was a real big cast, and working with Tommy [Howell] was great."

By the end of 1983, Kirk's career came to a screeching halt. Looking back now, he feels lucky that at the very young age of thirteen there was plenty to keep him occupied. Though he wanted to act again, he didn't want to go through the grind of auditioning and worrying about whether or not he'd won or lost roles. He had been very successful in the few short years he'd been working and had been incredibly let down when *Two Marriages* was canceled. After the work he'd done in preparing for his role and the advice he'd asked of his friend, Adam Rich, it was all gone in such a short time.

He decided after the show's cancellation that if he was ever to appear on another show, he would not allow himself to think about its ratings. "If I let my life revolve around the show being a hit, I'd only be setting myself up for disappointment later on," he commented during the first season of *Growing Pains*. "Of course, I hope people will watch this show and that it will stay on the air for a long time. But I know it's only natural for things to come to an end," he added.

He also knew that every actor struggles a little before hitting it big. And he knew he had more going for him than a lot of other young kids trying to act. He had his parents, for one thing, and their love and support meant everything to him. And he had the encouragement of a caring agent who envisioned a bright future for Kirk.

He took full advantage of his time spent away from work to concentrate on going to school and enjoying his first work-free summer. He knew he would return to acting, and he welcomed the time he had to himself.

His days were spent with his closest friends, whom he hadn't seen for the entire time he was filming *Two Marriages*. "I like going over to my friends' houses," he confides. "We like seeing movies, playing racquetball, and going to the beach."

His friends have always been very special to him, and he enjoyed spending time with them on the beach. But one day Kirk decided he was ready to audition again. The weeks with no work proved his determination to continue to strive in the career he now desperately wanted.

His really good friends gave him the sound advice he was waiting to hear. "You were really good in *Two Marriages*," encouraged one close friend. "Why don't you try to get on another show?"

Kirk thought long about acting again and decided to talk it over with his parents. Barbara didn't want to push her young son but knew that if he auditioned again, he was bound to win a good role.

She contacted his agent and told her that Kirk wanted to go on another tryout. While they waited for the agent to set up an audition or to tell Kirk of an open call, he began reading lines from old scripts he had saved. He was convinced that he would be able to land a bigger role this time if he just tried harder. The roles he'd had in TV movies hadn't satisfied him creatively. Though the parts had gotten bigger, he'd still been cast as the son of the lead character; a part with no story line of its own.

Now that he was seriously pursuing his career as an actor, he began to set higher goals for his future in the business. It was apparent that the reason he hadn't gotten bigger parts was the fact that he was still too young.

His age was keeping him from being offered the parts he knew he could play. Those parts were being portrayed by older actors, and Kirk, who had just turned fourteen, knew he had a long way to go.

The first sign of hope for Kirk came in the form of a movie entitled *The Best of Times*. He went to audition for the role of Teddy Hightower, the son of the character to be played by Kurt Russell. Kirk was excited but managed to keep his composure when reading for the part. After he spoke the few lines given to him, he was thanked, and left the large casting room.

Though he was again sent home with no definite answer, he felt especially confident about the entire audition. There were other boys his age in the running, but Kirk couldn't help but hope that maybe he'd be chosen. If he was the lucky one to play the part, he knew it would help him a great deal in the future. After all, it was a full-length feature film that not only starred Kurt Russell but Robin Williams as well, and Kirk dreamed of appearing on the big screen.

While Kirk waited to hear what the results were, his agent sent him on another audition for a new television show called *Growing Pains*. When Kirk found out that he would be reading for the role of Mike Seaver, the oldest son, in a thirty-minute family comedy, he was thrilled. Finally, after playing the youngest child in everything he had done, he was looking forward to trying out for a role he felt would have more potential.

After his TV audition, Kirk waited, wondered, and hoped for the best. He knew both parts would be good for his career and thought about which one he'd rather get, if he did indeed get one. He loved the idea of possibly appearing in a movie, but another weekly series also interested him.

After much thought he decided he couldn't choose between the two. He would wait, and he wouldn't think any further about either role. Instead, he went back to concentrating on school and going out with his friends.

Then one day the phone rang. It was Kirk's agent to tell him he had been cast in *The Best of Times*. Finally, Kirk thought, a part he could feel excited about. As he prepared for the shooting of the movie he studied his lines, speaking them to himself in front of a mirror to check his appearance. He spent so many hours rehearsing and reading over his part of Teddy Hightower that he didn't even think about the results of his other audition.

The character from *Growing Pains* crossed his mind one day, and just as it had entered his thoughts, the phone rang. The call brought good news concerning the role of Mike Seaver. Kirk had impressed the producers of the show with his spontaneity and flair for reading comedy, and they wanted him back to read for the director. It was the chance Kirk was hoping for.

As he eagerly wrote down the date and time of his second audition, he didn't know that one phone call was the beginning of something that would change his entire life.

3. *SCORING A TOUCHDOWN*

Nineteen eighty-five was a banner year for Kirk. His first feature film gave him enough acclaim to prove that he could hold the audiences of the big screen, as well as the small. Even though he began filming the first season of *Growing Pains* three months after he completed the filming of *The Best of Times*, it wasn't until later in the year that Kirk catapulted into the superstardom he is enjoying now.

Filming *The Best of Times*, studying his first scripts for *Growing Pains*, and going to school put the young actor on a tight schedule. He felt his priority, at that time, was to concentrate on his first feature film, *The Best of Times*, because he wanted to be sure he did everything right on the set. The character he portrayed, Teddy Hightower, was the son of an ex-football hero, played by Kurt Russell, and although his role was a supporting one, Kirk felt he was given the opportunity to display his acting abilities for moviegoing audiences. The film also starred comedian-turned-actor Robin Williams of *Mork and Mindy* fame, and Kirk found this experience very important to his growth as an actor. He took full advantage of learning as much as he could while working on the set.

At the time, teen magazines had begun to feature a still unknown Kirk as an upcoming teen heartthrob, and it was ironic that he was acting opposite Kurt Russell, whose own career had originally skyrocketed as a teen idol. Kirk sought the opportunity to ask Kurt as many questions as he could, and Russell, in return, spent a lot of time with him, offering his advice and explaining acting to this young, eager-to-learn boy.

Because of his blond hair, blue eyes, and clean-cut appearance, all the attention Kurt Russell received in his early years was basically from young girls who adored him. He appeared in all the teen magazines of the day and says he enjoyed receiving letters and meeting fans.

When Kurt saw that the same thing was happening to Kirk on the set of *The Best of Times*, it brought back memories of his own early success. The two got along famously and would talk for hours. Kurt made working fun for the new heartthrob who was playing his son, and Kirk appreciated all the advice Kurt Russell gave him.

As the star of the recent films *Silkwood*, *Escape from New York*, *The Thing*, *Swing Shift*, and *The Mean Season*, Kurt was a seasoned professional who had been working in the business for over twenty years. Kirk knew he was the best actor he could talk to about dealing with success and looked forward to every day of filming because he consistently learned something new.

He says he was glad his first part was small

because he was able to learn more by working with stars like Kurt Russell and Robin Williams. "Kurt played my dad in *The Best of Times*, so basically all my scenes were with him," reflects Kirk. "We had done a lot of shooting, and they had to cut some of my scenes out. I had been in more of the movie. But it was a great first experience for me. I learned so much from it."

As a fan of comedy, Kirk enjoyed working with Robin Williams. "He's the funniest guy on earth," he asserts. "He was constantly cracking jokes during filming. Sometimes he'd have me laughing so much I couldn't stop."

The Best of Times is the story of Jack Dundee, played to perfection by Robin wearing horn-rimmed glasses and short hair, and his high-school buddy, the star quarterback Reno Hightower, played by Kurt Russell. It begins with a football game at Taft High School in 1973 that would have awarded Taft its first football championship—if Dundee hadn't fumbled the ball.

Dundee is haunted by the game and continually runs the film of his momentous misplay. He is convinced that if the game is replayed, he will be able to win this time, make Taft the champs, and therefore rewrite history. Reno Hightower, who unlike his friend has put his high-school years behind him, opposes the idea at first. Eventually he agrees with his longtime buddy and former teammate, and the game is played with glorious results.

As the son of two high-school sweethearts, Kirk, as Teddy, finds himself being torn by his parents' failing marriage. His mother, played by Pamela Reed, desperately wants to get out of the rundown little Midwestern town, and his father, played by Russell, has to settle for working in an auto shop because all his football dreams were smashed when he graduated from high school. Jack Dundee finally pulls his friends together and, in turn, saves the Hightowers' marriage, as well as his own, which was suffering from his obsession with winning the football game.

The part of Teddy Hightower was both an interesting and a challenging one for Kirk to play. Realizing the pain that children of divorce go through, his emotions were put to the test to play this serious role. Kirk's home life is such a happy one, and his parents are so much in love, that it was impossible for him to draw on real-life experiences to play Teddy. Even though it seemed as if there was a major difference between Kirk and his character, the young actor asserts, "Teddy was still just a kid who loved sports and his mom and dad, despite the problems he was going through."

Not only would Kirk's first film, *The Best of Times*, soon open, but he would also begin filming *Growing Pains*, the show that would make him a superstar. He remained modest about his sudden success, even though he was now in the spotlight. From the beginning he didn't want to be treated differently because he was an actor.

One incident that stands out in his mind upset him greatly. His oldest sister, Bridgette, had become friends with a new girl at school. They were close friends for a while and went shopping on Saturdays and spent hours on the phone. One day Bridgette realized that her friend kept asking questions about

Kirk, and it was obvious that all she wanted was to meet Bridgette's now famous brother. It upset Kirk to think that someone would fake a friendship with one of his sisters just because he was an actor.

"My family doesn't like that at all," he says. "Even though it only happened one time, I've learned who my friends are, and so have my sisters."

Kirk is very specific when it comes to friendship. "To me a friend is someone I can trust," he offers. "Someone who will tell me the truth and will give me advice if I need it. That's the way I am, and I would expect my friends to be the same."

He remained close to the boys he grew up with, but he has recently become friends with fellow actors Jason Bateman and Ricky Schroder. Jason and Ricky are both popular teen stars, and as the new kid on the block, Kirk enjoys talking to them about acting and their popularity. The threesome love going to the beach and playing racquetball when they can break away from their busy schedules.

Kirk admires Jason's and Ricky's work and admits that he would love to do a movie with them someday. Though they love to talk about acting, they don't let it cut into their time to have fun. When they get together, they usually play racquetball, a game all three list as their favorite.

"Whenever I get time to spend with friends, I usually like to go to the beach or see a movie too," Kirk adds. He says being friends with Jason and Ricky is different because, like him, they are in the business and understand that sometimes work is a priority.

"Sometimes it's hard," reflects Kirk. "When I'm

working, I'm not able to go out and do what I like to do on weekends. My parents have always been there for me to drive me wherever I want to go. That makes it easier for me to spend time with my friends."

Kirk was amazed by the fact that both Jason and Ricky were teen idols, and he would ask them countless questions about how they felt to be admired by so many girls.

What he didn't know at the time was that soon he would be the top teen idol in the country and would know exactly what the honor felt like.

4. *INSTANT STARDOM*

When Kirk Cameron arrived at the Warner Brothers television studio to read for a new show called *Growing Pains,* he never thought he had much of a chance of getting the role. He wasn't even sure how successful the show might be.

Kirk was sent on the audition by his agent on a hunch, even though it was known that the producers were looking for someone four years older than Kirk. Still, he was encouraged to give it a try.

The show's premise was in the tradition of *Family Ties* and *The Cosby Show,* in which the situation comedy centered around an American family for thirty minutes. It is complete with the fun and exuberance of the trials and tribulations of an eighties family. In early 1985, producers Michael Sullivan, Dan Guntzelman, and Steve Marshall began auditioning actors to fill the roles of the Seaver family.

Kirk's agent called to say that she'd set up an audition for him. The character he would be reading for was the oldest boy in the Seaver family: a mischievous teenager who was super-cool and wisecracking at the same time.

At fourteen Kirk was maturing, but he still had an appealing innocence about him. The audition was like the usual interview. He submitted his résumé, was handed a script, and was asked to look it over. After flipping anxiously through the script, he was then asked by Sullivan to turn to a certain page and read what was marked off. Kirk stood very still and studied the words on the page. As he began to read the words he suddenly stopped and started laughing at the humorous writing.

This impressed the producers, since no one before Kirk had enjoyed himself so much. Though they knew he didn't have the formal television training they were looking for, Sullivan thought Kirk was a natural. However, for now, he told him, "Thank you, we'll be in touch," and allowed him to leave.

Weeks went by. In the meantime the producers auditioned others, but Sullivan couldn't get Kirk out of his mind. At his young age Kirk possessed a fresh quality, and Sullivan knew he was exactly what he was looking for to play Mike Seaver. He convinced Guntzelman and Marshall to call Kirk back for a second audition. This time Kirk would be reading for the director of the show.

Because Kirk's only prior television credit was *Two Marriages*, where he had played a dramatic role, the director was skeptical about whether or not he could handle comedy. Kirk's reading of the always clever and effervescently comical Mike Seaver convinced the director he was capable of playing the role.

Unfortunately the young actor was sent home with the same burning question—Do I have the part? He wondered why they never told him anything on the spot, why they always had to notify him of his success or failure at some future time. He left the studio feeling uncertain of the outcome.

For the next few days Kirk bided his time, and soon a second callback was arranged. He thought his chances looked good this time, even though he was frightened that it all might be left up in the air once again.

The third reading took place before fifteen ABC network executives, and at first Kirk was very nervous. He had never auditioned for so many people at once, and just the thought of it overwhelmed him. He knew they would be judging the way he spoke every word, so he decided to put it out of his mind. He read the lines with a fetching blend of conviction and humor and went home, again with no answer.

A few days later the telephone rang with the good news. "Kirk," his agent began, "are you ready to hear the outcome of your *Growing Pains* auditions?"

Kirk shrugged and answered, "Yes."

"You did it!" the agent shouted. "You got the part of Mike Seaver!"

Kirk was suddenly catapulted into the loftiest state of ecstasy that he had ever known. "Fantastic," he exclaimed with a grin that spread from ear to ear.

He was to begin rehearsals the first week in June, and he couldn't wait to get back on a television show. He had enjoyed working on *Two Marriages* so much, he missed the day-to-day excitement of rehearsing and filming a family show.

Growing Pains was created by Neal Marlens, who named his fictional Seaver family after Tom Seaver, the famous New York Mets pitcher. Says Joanna Kerns, who plays Maggie Seaver, "The creator of our show is a big Mets fan. That's why our name is Seaver and our neighbors are the Koosmans. If you listen closely, we talk often about Long Island, Syosset, and Huntington."

Growing Pains premiered to an eager audience on Tuesday, September 24, 1985, and was an instant hit. The show's success was partly due to its refreshing look at family life in the eighties. As the audience was introduced to the Seaver family that fall evening at 8:30 P.M., Maggie Seaver was returning to her former job as a newspaper reporter after fifteen years.

As she was going back to work, her husband Jason (played by Alan Thicke) was moving his psychiatric practice into their home so he could be there for his three children. Though Maggie keeps her job, she continues to worry about repercussions on the domestic front. She misses her kids and wonders whether her husband hasn't taken on more than he can manage.

Idealistic Jason's confidence that he and the children share a good understanding occasionally wavers in the day-to-day skirmishes of managing sixteen-year-old Mike, who wants more freedom but not more responsibility; fifteen-year-old Carol, too precocious for her own good; and ten-year-old Ben, who is close to his mother and wishes she was still at home. Though the role of Carol was originally portrayed by another actress in the pilot, it was recast and given to Tracey Gold for the series. The youngest son, Ben, is played by Jeremy Miller, who is best known for lending his voice muscles to the role of Linus in the animated *Peanuts* specials.

The early success of *Growing Pains* convinced Michael Sullivan that he had done the right thing in casting Kirk in the role of the oldest Seaver boy. Executive producers Dan Guntzelman and Steve Marshall agreed. Kirk brought a natural and spontaneous approach to a seemingly unlikable character, making him charming instead of obnoxious.

As the show gained a larger audience Kirk began to catch the attention of girls everywhere. Without expecting it, he was becoming an idol to them, and letters began pouring into the offices of ABC and Warner Brothers.

At the same time his photo began appearing on the covers of major teen magazines, but the process was a slow but sure buildup for the then fifteen-year-old actor.

One teen editor said of Kirk, "We knew he had something about him that was going to appeal to teenagers. He had a special look, and we began running small pictures of him on our magazine covers. We wanted every kid in the country to know all about him, hoping we'd get a response from them."

The response the magazines began to receive was overwhelming as the demand for Kirk grew. He instantly became the hottest young actor on television, and headlines in magazines started blasting notices like: "Look out, Michael J. Fox! Here comes Kirk Cameron!"

As a young boy just beginning to embark on an

acting career, Kirk hadn't anticipated such a rapid response to his work. With more and more girls buying teen magazines because of Kirk, it was clear to see that other teen idols like Ralph Macchio, Rob Lowe, and Michael J. Fox were being pushed aside to make way for Kirk. Finally kids everywhere had someone their own age they could relate to, unlike older idols. Kirk enjoyed all the early attention he received.

The Cameron family traveled with Kirk for his first publicity tour to the East Coast. It was his first opportunity to meet people who watched the show and to speak to the press, who had started featuring him in their periodicals. It was also the first time since his trip to Switzerland that he would be on a plane, and that was exciting to him. He would say later, "It amazes me how those things stay in the air."

Barbara kept a watchful eye on her son to be sure all the attention he was receiving wasn't going to his head. Both she and Robert were concerned that at such a young age Kirk might change because of his success. They soon came to realize that while he was enjoying the attention he was receiving, nothing was going to change this down-to-earth young man.

"When I started on *Growing Pains*, a few things changed at home," he professes. "But there really hasn't been one major change. It isn't like we had this regular routine that we lived by, and suddenly nothing was the same because I was on the show. We just shifted over a little bit and did what had to be done."

One of the only things that has affected the Camerons is the fact that while Kirk is working, they are unable to sit down and have the family dinner they were always so used to. On Tuesday nights, especially, when the show is taped before a live audience, Kirk is sometimes so excited that he only eats something very light. He is well aware of the fact that his career has placed further responsibilities on his parents and sisters, and he appreciates all the loving guidance they are giving him.

As he was asked to make more and more public appearances, his parents accompanied him everywhere. His successful career gave Kirk and his family the chance to travel to places they had never seen before.

"We didn't do much traveling outside of California before the show," asserts Kirk. "But now we're getting the opportunity to see cities we never thought we'd visit."

On one of his first stops at a press conference in New York City, the young actor said, beaming, "My entire family's thrilled for me. They love the fact that I'm on the show."

Kirk received an enormous amount of attention on his first tour, but much to everyone's amazement, his family was getting just as much attention. When they all went to Pennsylvania for Kirk's appearance at a car show, excited fans not only asked for Kirk's autograph but for the autographs of his parents and sisters as well. Kirk told one reporter, "My family is really having fun with all this."

Kirk was glad that his career was going so well, and because his mother had worked so hard to get him where he was, he wanted to show her that everything she did had been worth it.

"My career wouldn't be possible if it wasn't for the support of my parents," Kirk admits. "Because I'm still young, they have a lot to do with my decisions. I honestly believe that if they hadn't been behind me all the way when I was first starting out, I never would have gone into acting."

Robert and Barbara have always been there for Kirk. His mom spends her days on the set of the show whenever he's filming to make sure that he isn't taken advantage of at his young age. She makes sure he gets just as much time to study his schoolwork as he does to learn his lines. Kirk's parents are always there for their young son, to provide him with the guidance he's needed to get through the ups and downs of developing and maintaining a career.

While his mother advises her son on which projects he should or shouldn't accept, his father acts as his business manager, taking care of his money and taxes.

"My parents have really been an inspiration to me," says Kirk. "Especially my mom. She's really encouraged my career. I wouldn't be able to accept any acting jobs without talking with Mom and Dad first, and asking what they thought of it."

Although Kirk is still too young to make contract decisions without his parents, he says with conviction, "I think I'll always go to them even when I get older. I respect their judgment, and I know they'll always guide me in the right direction."

Kirk feels his parents are the most influential

people in his life. His sensitivity, responsibility, and sincerity stems from his mother, while his father, a schoolteacher who once taught math to junior-high-school students, endowed him with a keen sense for business. Kirk has inherited his father's mathematical ability. His grades remain high in that subject, but science ranks as Kirk's favorite in school.

"I've always been very interested in science and biology," he confesses. As a young boy, Kirk's first ambition was to become a doctor. He is very serious about keeping his grades in school high, because it's a goal he still hasn't totally abandoned.

During Kirk's publicity tour, he and his sisters were accompanied by a tutor. Between all the interviews, press conferences, and photo sessions, Kirk always found time for his assignments, and made sure his sisters studied their schoolwork as well.

Just before he began his stint on *Growing Pains*, Kirk had been a straight-A student at Lawrence Junior High School right near the Camerons' beautiful home in the San Fernando Valley, and his education meant too much to him to slack off. He continued to work hard because he plans on going to college and wants to be sure his grades remain high. Being privately tutored has helped him tremendously to achieve his original goal toward a full education.

"I like to study by myself," he says with confidence. "That's the best way for me to learn. But if I do need help with something, I'm not afraid to ask for it."

Since the show requires a full day of rehearsing and blocking (setting the movement of the actors on the set), a tutor is also brought in for Kirk, Tracey, and Jeremy. "Jeremy is younger, so he has his own tutor, but Kirk and I are taught by Ben Friedman," says Tracey Gold, who graduated from high school in June 1987. The hours for rehearsing the show are from ten in the morning until seven-thirty at night. "Everyone usually gets to the studio at ten," Tracey explains. "But Kirk, Jeremy, and I all get there at eight so we can get in two hours of school."

A total of three hours a day for education is required by law for child actors, and it is very important for these three young stars to study hard. They usually have to make up the hours they lose during filming by studying at night or on the weekends.

"Usually we get the assignments from our regular school," notes Kirk. "And we work on them with our tutor. The grades are then averaged into the ones we receive in our regular classroom."

For many teenagers their work at school is enough to keep them busy. It would seem that, when combined, working and concentrating on school are very difficult tasks for these young actors. But Kirk and his two costars are very determined about what they do. They are able to study their schoolwork and their lines with ease. And their dedication in both has paid off, as all three are superb actors as well as honor students.

A typical week on the set of *Growing Pains* begins on a Wednesday morning when the cast is handed the script for a new episode. All day Wednesday, Thursday and Friday they rehearse the show.

During these days the cast is able to wear their own clothes. Kirk likes dressing in T-shirts and jeans because they are the easiest for him to move around in.

During working hours the cast always finds time to have fun and clown around. "We have a lot of fun while we're working," says Tracey Gold. "Everyone is always playing jokes on someone else, and I think most of the jokes are played on me because I'm the most gullible," she adds, laughing.

Once in a while Kirk will bring one of his pet snakes to the set. He likes to kid Joanna with it because she promptly leaves the room every time she sees it. Kirk is a cutup who is always quick with a funny line. Even while he's performing, if something in the script strikes him funny, he will stop and laugh, usually breaking up the entire cast.

The cast goes over their lines together, and they always offer advice about how a scene should be played and what each character should say. After all, no one is closer to the characters than the actors portraying them.

Kirk, especially, loves playing smart-aleck Mike Seaver. "I really can relate to Mike because he's a typical, cool teenager," he says. "Sometimes he's a bit too confident, but he's pretty close to the way I am. He's a wise guy but also has a great sense of humor. I think of him in terms of being like a car salesman. He can talk his way out of anything."

On Friday night a complete run-through of the show is performed before producers and network executives so they can get a general idea of what the episode for that week will look like. "We begin rehearsals around a table and just read the lines," explains Kirk. "By Friday night we get into costume, and the director stages exactly where we have to stand for each scene."

By Tuesday the cast and crew have a good idea of what the show will be and what needs to be perfected. On Tuesday night Stage 30 on the Warner Brothers Ranch is open to the public. The cast arrives on the set early in the afternoon for more run-throughs, and by six o'clock that evening, they are sent backstage so the studio audience can take their seats.

"We do the show all day without an audience," says Tracey. "It's done very, very slowly with all the details. By the end of the day we're ready for the actual filming at night."

At six-thirty a large crowd is allowed into the huge soundstage. On the stage before them is a row of sets connected to each other. They are the different parts of the Seaver house, and any other sets needed for the episode being filmed. As the excitement builds, a man walks out and stands at center stage.

He begins talking to the audience, telling jokes, revealing little-known facts about the cast, and answering questions. "What is Kirk really like?" is called out to him, and with a smile he yells back, "Terrific!"

The time the audience spends inside the studio is a thrilling experience, and they are often unaware that the taping takes approximately two hours. "Anyone who comes to a show has to expect to be in there for a while," Tracey comments. "It takes a lot longer than a half hour to film each show."

By seven o'clock the cast is ready to take their places; the action slowly begins. "There is a lot to have memorized by Tuesday night," says Kirk. "And there is always something happening that isn't supposed to. There is never a show that goes by without somebody messing up."

When their show is wrapped up, the cast always comes out to talk to the audience. "I just want to take this time to thank you all for coming," Alan Thicke announces while the rest of the cast waves to the studio audience cheering and applauding them. Kirk doesn't like to disappoint the fans who have come to see him and always talks to them. Sometimes he even shakes hands and personally thanks them for coming.

When the actors leave the stage, the lights in the studio brighten and the audience slowly files out. Most of them go home, satisfied to have just seen the actual taping of a top-ten show. However, a select group gather by the backstage door. They want to see their favorite actors close-up and take home an autograph as a souvenir.

As the backstage door swings open, crew members straggle out. The excitement can be felt. Questions like, "When is Kirk coming out?" begin to be asked. No one seems to know. In the meantime Alan and Joanna sign autographs, Jeremy poses for photographs, and Tracey talks a bit about her successful career.

The entire cast makes sure that everyone who takes the time to wait for them at the backstage door is satisfied. Tracey says sincerely, "I don't mind stopping and signing autographs after the show at all. In fact, I really like it."

Kirk likes it too. When the door opens and he walks out, he is bombarded with pens and pieces of paper and gladly signs his name for fans. "I think of it as a reward for the work I do. It shows how much people care," Kirk says, but he does admit that there are times when being so recognizable is inconvenient.

"I was in a restaurant once, and the crowds that began to gather outside and near my table became so chaotic, I was asked to leave," he confides. Kirk now must keep a low profile when he goes out. Because he is so popular, it seems that whenever he wants to enjoy a day at the beach or ride his bicycle, he is easily recognized and stopped.

Kirk had never expected to receive such a response from so many young fans. Before he ascended to stardom, he would be stopped once in a while and asked to sign an autograph or two. But the last thing he thought would happen were the scores of girls who wait patiently for him at the studio and scream when he walks out.

"When I first started on the show, I couldn't believe all the people who waited outside and wanted my autograph," Kirk admits.

He has always been close to his fans and likes talking to them, signing autographs and acknowledging everyone who has come to meet him. "I don't look at them as fans," Kirk says. "To me they're like friends. All they want is to be friendly, and I'll always go out of my way to show my appreciation."

Sometimes a few fans will get overexcited at the sight of their idol. There have been some occasions when Kirk has been mobbed by girls swooning and tugging at him. Kirk knows they don't mean to hurt him, that they are just thrilled to see him in person. He realizes that if they tug at his clothes, all they want is a piece of him to take home as a souvenir. But because of these scenes he has had to give up going to places he would like to go—where he might see—and be seen by—his many fans.

"If I want to go out, sometimes I'll put on a big hat and jacket, and not too many people will know it's me," he confesses. But his disguise didn't always help him, and privacy became a rarity for Kirk as his popularity grew.

He remembers when he went to Disneyland with his family right about the time that *Growing Pains* was making him a star. It didn't take long before a few girls spotted him enjoying the Disneyland attractions.

"It was fun in the beginning," says Kirk. "But after a while there was this group of girls who kept following us everywhere we went. Every time I turned around, they were there."

Although Kirk sometimes wishes he could have a day all to himself without having fans "ambush" him, he is very concerned about the impression he gives. He doesn't want anyone to think he is stuck-up. It hurts him when people assume he has an attitude problem because he is a celebrity. Anyone who knows Kirk knows that he isn't like that at all.

"I don't like it when people who don't know me think I'm a certain way because I'm an actor," he says. "When it does happen, I'm careful that I don't do anything to make them think I'm stuck-up."

On October 12, 1985, Kirk celebrated his fifteenth birthday. One reporter asked him how he was handling his instant stardom, and he answered, "Well, it's a lot of work. But I'm handling it just fine."

The following month Kirk was honored at the Seventh Annual Youth-in-Film Awards. He won his trophy for Best Actor in a New Television Series and was ecstatic over it. "When my name was called, I didn't know what to say," he confessed later. "I just sat there for a few minutes, not realizing that I had actually won." His costars Tracey Gold and Jeremy Miller were also the recipients of Best Newcomer Awards, and *Growing Pains* itself was awarded Best New Show.

On the night of the ceremony Kirk escorted pretty Ami Dolenz, daughter of the Monkees' Micky Dolenz. Kirk looked handsome in his tuxedo and enjoyed attending his first real formal party. Photos of Kirk and Ami together appeared in magazines, and rumors about the cute twosome began to run rampant. Ami was the first girl he had asked to a Hollywood function, and he insisted to reporters, "Ami and I are just great friends. Right now there is no special girl in my life."

As the holidays approached in late 1985, Kirk was especially happy and regarded Christmas that year as a very special day. "Christmas has always been my favorite holiday," Kirk says. "It has always been a real happy time for my whole family." It seemed, however, that it was especially joyous for the Cameron clan that year.

With *Growing Pains* at the top of the ratings, it

Kirk with
close friend and
co-star Jeremy
Miller.
PHOTO BY
SCOTT DOWNIE/
CELEBRITY PHOTO.

Kirk and Alan Thicke clown on the set of Growing Pains.
PHOTO BY PHOTO TRENDS.

A striking pose of the Seaver kids. Left to right, Jeremy Miller, Tracey Gold, and Kirk.
PHOTO BY PHOTO TRENDS.

The Growing Pains family. Top, left to right, Kirk, Joanna Kerns, *and* Tracey Gold; *Bottom, left to right,* Alan Thicke *and* Jeremy Miller.

PHOTO BY PHOTO TRENDS.

Cleveland
Metroparks
Zoo Director
Chuck Varacek
introduces Kirk
to Lucy, an 80
pound python.
PHOTO BY
JANET MACOSKA/
STAR FILE.

Kirk with one of his pet snakes.
PHOTO BY JANET MACOSKA/ STAR FILE.

Kirk's sisters, left to right, Candace, Bridgette, and Melissa, share his home-baked muffins.

Kirk with his mother, Barbara.
PHOTO BY ROBIN PLATZER/IMAGES.

On the set of his new movie, Like Father, Like Son, Kirk takes a break to sign autographs for fans.

PHOTO BY VINNIE ZUFFANTE/ STAR FILE.

Kirk filming his new movie, Like Father, Like Son, at John Byrd Junior High School in Sun Valley, California.
PHOTO BY STAR FILE.

Kirk is the spokesperson for the "You're Souper Just the Way You Are" campaign sponsored by Campbell's Kids' Soups. PHOTO BY ROBIN PLATZER/IMAGES.

Kirk with the Campbell's Kids at the "You're Souper Just the Way You Are" campaign.
PHOTO BY ROBIN PLATZER/IMAGES.

Kirk in an airport leaving for Dallas, Texas.
PHOTO BY JANET GOUGH/ CELEBRITY PHOTO.

Kirk arrives at an ABC party.

PHOTO BY
SCOTT DOWNIE/
CELEBRITY PHOTO.

Kirk goes over his script in the car before arriving on the set of Growing Pains.
PHOTO BY VINNIE ZUFFANTE/ STAR FILE.

The star of
Growing Pains.
PHOTO BY
VINNIE ZUFFANTE/
STAR FILE.

appeared that the show was going to have a long and auspicious run, and Kirk looked forward to what the new year would bring. But for the time being, he was enjoying every happy moment spent with his family and friends.

As the new year was welcomed into the Cameron home, Kirk thought ahead to 1986. Already a star on TV, he wondered if he would be able to break into movies and go beyond *Growing Pains*. He had enjoyed the work he did for his first movie, *The Best of Times*, and thought ahead of someday doing another full-length feature film. He loved everything that was happening to him. Kirk is not the kind of actor who takes things like fame and money and being a star too seriously. He just feels lucky to be doing something he really enjoys. The new year was going to be interesting for Kirk, and he was eagerly awaiting what direction his career would be going in.

When he was asked during an interview to explain *Growing Pains* and why he thinks it's so popular, he said, "The show is very realistic. I think that people want to see the family unit back together—surviving all the pressures. That's one of the reasons I think *Growing Pains* is such a success."

Though Kirk was aware of the fact that *Growing Pains* had become an instant hit with viewers, he hadn't yet grasped the fact that he was one of the major reasons for its success. This would be proven to him in the months ahead.

5. *TOP TEENAGE HEARTTHROB*

" I like to see myself in magazines, even though some of my friends tease me about it," said Kirk Cameron during an interview in 1986. Reflecting further about all the attention he was beginning to receive, he explained, "Most of my friends don't expect to open up a magazine and see me as a pinup. They know I'm an actor, but to them I'm still just Kirk."

To millions of others, however, Kirk has become the top teenage heartthrob in the country. His face now graces the covers of countless magazines, and Kirk has exclaimed that everything that happened in just one year's time was "a dream come true."

As the demand for him grew, Kirk's many admirers wanted to know everything about him. One question often asked is how he feels about his fans. "I love them all," he answers with enthusiasm.

"When I first began getting a few letters, I sat down and read every one," confides Kirk. "And I answered every one because it was very important to me to send a response to the girls who took the time to write to me."

When the mail began to pour in by the thousands, Kirk at first considered hiring a fan-mail answering service, but his family wouldn't hear of it. Instead the Camerons decided to read and answer all of Kirk's mail themselves.

"We sorted out all the letters, and little by little we began answering them," says Robert. "Kirk was receiving mail from all over the world. Some of the fans didn't even know the show. They had just seen his picture in a magazine and decided to write to tell him how much they really liked what he said in a certain article. These girls really care about Kirk, and we care about them to send them some kind of response to their letters," he added with sincerity.

The mail for Kirk continued to pour into the offices at ABC and Warner Brothers. Eventually it was counted and totaled at two thousand letters a day. Upon reading some of his letters, Kirk comments, "The girls who write to me are really nice. They take the time to tell me everything about themselves. And I really am grateful for every letter I get."

The Camerons put a family effort into mailing out photos and letters to the fans who bombard Kirk with mail. "With all this going on, I had gotten the idea to start a fan club for Kirk," says his mother, Barbara, who now runs the Kirk Cameron Fan Club out of a room in the family's home.

With such a rapid response from fans wanting to join, the Cameron family found themselves working full-time sending out fan-club kits. The kit includes a large assortment of Kirk items, such as a school folder with his photo on both sides, two 8" × 10" black-and-white glossies, four black-and-white wallet-size photos, one 22″ × 17″ folded autographed color poster, a color membership card, a picture button, and an unauthorized biography. Also being sold separately is a Kirk T-shirt and a pillowcase with his photo printed on one side.

In only a few months over seven thousand loving Kirk Cameron fans joined his club. "It's fantastic," marvels Barbara. "We never expected this many people to join in such a short time."

To show how much he cares about his fans, Kirk became involved with the Just Say No to Drugs campaign. "I feel it's important for me to tell kids to stay away from drugs," he says. "I'm a teenager, and I'm hoping, since I am the same age, kids will listen to me."

Last year he suggested to the writers of *Growing Pains* that he wanted to send a personal message to his fans on the dangers of drug abuse. Interested in his request, they optioned to create an entire episode in which his character, Mike Seaver, is pressured by his peers to take drugs at a party.

The controversial episode concerned network executives who decided early on not to air it. Because Kirk was so popular with teenagers everywhere and represented what they felt was a wholesome quality, they didn't like suggesting the subject of drugs on a family television show like *Growing Pains.*

The cast felt differently. Since drugs are a problem on all levels of society today, they couldn't understand why the Seaver family would be excluded from it. They tried to convince the network executives that the reason they made the show in the first place was to discourage kids from using drugs.

"We all fought hard to get that show on the air," says Tracey. "Because we all felt so strongly about the importance of it."

With the constant persuasion of producers Mike Sullivan, Dan Guntzelman, and Steven Marshall, as well as the concerned cast who wanted it on the air, the network finally agreed. On Tuesday, February 10, a special episode of *Growing Pains* was aired on national television. Its meaning was powerful, and teenagers were inspired by Kirk's concern with the subject of drug abuse.

At the end of the show Kirk stepped out of character to address the audience with a personalized message about the drug problem. "I want everyone to know that it isn't cool to take drugs," he said. Kirk would later comment, "This show was very important to me. I want everyone to know you *can* say no to drugs. I feel very strongly about this problem, and I can't understand why kids would want to take drugs. I hope that Just Say No to Drugs campaign is helping."

As an advocate of the Just Say No to Drugs campaign, Kirk has done all he could to discourage teenagers against getting involved with drugs. He also appears in the Don't Do Drugs television commercials that are mounted by ABC. Knowing the importance of these spots and his guest appearances, Kirk makes sure he fits time into his busy schedule to do everything he is asked.

On May 9, 1987, he traveled with his costar Tracey Gold to Chicago, Illinois, to host the Just Say No to

Drugs parade down Wilbur Street. At the time Kirk was in the middle of filming a movie, *Like Father, Like Son,* and thought at first that he wasn't going to have the time to appear. But the campaign is too important to him.

"I'm having a great time. I'm really happy to be here," Kirk said, smiling. "I want everyone to know how I feel about drugs. That's why I'm here today. I think everyone out there should realize that we don't need drugs to be cool. We had a great reaction last year on a special *Growing Pains* episode when we showed everyone that drugs are not cool."

As Kirk announced the marchers in the parade he waved, winked, and smiled at all the girls screaming his name. He was sorry he couldn't stay more than an hour, but he had to get back to Los Angeles to continue work on his movie, *Like Father, Like Son.*

Before he left, he stared right into the camera and said, "I think everyone should remember we're all out here today for one thing, and that is to say no to drugs."

The subject of drugs isn't the only thing Kirk feels strongly about. He is also opposed to smoking, and last year he single-handedly tried to ban smoking from the set of *Growing Pains.*

Because he is so health conscious, he was concerned with the amount of smoke he was inhaling every day while rehearsing. He voiced his opinion about how harmful it is and tried to put an end to smoking on the soundstage.

Although it was done with a feeling of concern, Kirk wound up offending too many smokers on the set. In the end a compromise was agreed upon, and the soundstage was divided into smoking and non-smoking sections. Kirk was satisfied; at least he felt he had accomplished something.

Kirk is a sensitive, down-to-earth young man who proves that he really cares about teenagers his age. In November 1986, Campbell's Kids' Soups sponsored a program to help kids develop self-esteem. The program, called "You're Souper the Way You Are," offers advice to young people everywhere on the importance of self-respect and liking themselves.

As the top teen heartthrob, Kirk was the obvious choice to be the spokesperson of this program. "When Campbell's Kids' Soups told me about their latest cause, I was very interested," says Kirk. "The message of the whole program is for kids like myself to feel good about themselves."

He agreed to be the program's spokesperson and traveled with his mother to the Children's Museum of Manhattan to launch the national program. He spent a day talking to New York City school-children, explaining to them how important it is for them to like themselves because "if you don't, it affects everything you do and feel."

This cause was only one of the many Kirk wanted to participate in. He is very modest about his success; he isn't the type to take his celebrity status too seriously. Instead he uses his popularity as a means to help others. Whenever the opportunity arises, Kirk is ready to lend his support to any worthwhile cause.

"I've been asked to be involved with many different causes," Kirk reflects. "Unfortunately I have to turn down some of them because there is just no time in my schedule."

He did find time for the Juvenile Diabetes Bike-A-Thon sponsored by McDonald's. He and the rest of the *Growing Pains* cast were among ten thousand Californians to participate in the fight against diabetes. The bike-a-thon held a soft spot in Kirk's heart because one of his best friends, Brennan Thicke (Alan's son), has diabetes. In fact, Alan has done so much for the Juvenile Diabetes Foundation that they honored him at one of their events. Both Alan and Kirk are very dedicated to their charitable work, almost as dedicated as they are to acting.

As Kirk's popularity grew, producers took notice of him. In 1986, he and Alan were asked to host the show, *Friday Night Videos*. It was the first time Kirk appeared on television as himself.

He enjoys making guest appearances on television shows. When Bob Hope celebrated his eighty-fourth birthday with a three-hour special, Kirk was honored when he was asked to take part in it.

Besides his extra-added television exposure, Kirk was also invited to the Mardi Gras celebration in New Orleans, Louisiana. He was dressed in a gorgeous white suit and was thrilled to be part of the Mardi Gras.

"I'd always heard so much about this, and I've always wanted to go," Kirk said. "I'm very happy to be here."

The city was happy to have him there, and to prove it they honored him by declaring one of the days of his visit as Kirk Cameron Day.

Everything was happening so fast for Kirk. With

his TV show, *Growing Pains*, being serialized into a novel, and Kirk appearing as the cover story in *TV Guide*, now Kirk was being honored with his own day at the Mardi Gras celebration.

The thing that made these events even more exciting was that Kirk felt the year already belonged to him.

6. *THE* GROWING PAINS *FAMILY*

There must be times when Kirk Cameron feels fortunate to be working with such an easygoing ensemble of costars. "It would be real hard to get up every morning and go to the set if I didn't get along with the people I worked with," he says. "I honestly don't think I'd be able to act if I was under any kind of tension."

Luckily the cast and crew get along just fine. Of course, there is an occasional disagreement during working hours, but it doesn't last too long. "We're really like a family," observes Kirk. "We may argue once in a while, but we're real close."

Alan Thicke, who plays Jason Seaver on *Growing Pains*, echoes Kirk's words and adds, "I don't know how I'd survive on a show if we were all at each other's throats. I'm not an experienced enough actor to walk on the set and shrug off bad feelings."

Growing Pains is Alan's comeback after his unsuccessful experience as a late-night host on the short-lived talk show, *Thicke of the Night.*

Joanna Kerns who plays Maggie Seaver displays her own brand of humor to the working mother she portrays on *Growing Pains.* "I guess I could relate to Maggie because she's a lot like me," she offers. "We are both working mothers trying to devote an equal amount of attention to our work as well as our family. I just wish I could solve my problems in twenty-two minutes like we do on the show," she adds realistically.

Joanna's daughter, Ashley, is always on the set and has become close friends with Jeremy Miller, who plays the youngest Seaver son Ben. Jeremy is a bright, eleven-year-old boy whose success story parallels Kirk's. Jeremy was discovered by a casting agent when he was a mere three years old and was led into a string of unforgettable commercials.

From the commercials came roles on TV's *Diff'rent Strokes* and *Punky Brewster*, and Jeremy's early exposure to television made him realize that he wants "to be an actor all my life. It's just something I really love," he says.

Jeremy, who is in the sixth grade, shares many hobbies with his onscreen brother, Kirk Cameron. They both love video games, skateboarding, and bike riding, and the two are as close off the set as they are on. "I have a ball when I'm with Kirk," says Jeremy. "He's so much fun, always telling a joke."

The only girl in the Seaver family is played by Tracey Gold. Tracey, who has three sisters in real life, loves the idea of having two brothers on *Growing Pains*. "I've never had brothers," she says. "And Kirk and Jeremy are like real brothers to me because we're so close. I feel very protective of Jeremy because he's younger. I know some people who don't have brothers or sisters and I feel I now have both," she adds, giggling.

Born in New York and raised in California, Tracey grew up in an acting family. Her younger sister, Missy, who portrayed Katie on *Benson,* has been on TV for most of her childhood, and their father, Harry, now an agent, began his career as an actor.

At age four, Tracey landed her first part in a television commercial. She has accumulated an impressive list of credits to her name, including fifteen TV movies, two feature films (*The Best of Times* with Kirk and *Shoot the Moon* with Diane Keaton) and two television series. Her first was *Goodnight Beantown* in 1983, and Tracey won the Youth-in-Film Best Actress award for her role in that show. Her second TV series, *Growing Pains,* also garnered a Youth-in-Film award for the young star in 1985.

Though Tracey fits the part of Carol Seaver perfectly, she wasn't hired on the spot. In fact, another actress appeared in the show's pilot. When the producers called Tracey to read for the role again, she was visiting her mother and sister in Chicago. She and her father flew to Los Angeles on Sunday for a Monday morning audition.

"After I read that Monday, they called me back on Saturday to work with the director," Tracey recalls. "And I went back the following Monday to read again. By the following Wednesday I was already reading for the network."

That Wednesday proved to be a big day for Tracey Gold. She arrived at the studio early in the morning and waited in the large casting room with a few other girls, also reading for the role of Carol Seaver. Tracey read her lines, and when she was finished, she went home. "To tell you the truth," she says honestly, "at that point it didn't make a difference whether I got the part or not."

That afternoon the phone rang in the Gold home and Tracey's dad answered it. "Hello, I'm calling from ABC publicity," the voice said. "We need Tracey's biography."

Harry stood solemnly, holding the receiver. "What are you talking about?" he asked.

"Didn't anyone tell you?" answered the publicity director. "Tracey got the part on *Growing Pains.*"

"Are you serious?" he asked in disbelief, and called Tracey downstairs.

In a matter of a few minutes the director phoned to tell Tracey the good news. He told her to get to the studio as fast as she could because a photographer was waiting for her.

"Before I knew it," says Tracey excitedly, "I was taking publicity stills for *TV Guide.*"

She says of Kirk, "He's great. There isn't anything else I could say about him. I worked with him two times before *Growing Pains*, and he makes working fun. He's got a great sense of humor."

Though Tracey and Kirk are now treated like stars, she reveals, "I don't know, nothing has changed for us. I've known Kirk for a long time. We live near each other, and I'm friends with his sisters. To me he's just Kirk and I'm just Tracey."

The friendship Kirk and Tracey share offscreen is probably the reason why they are so easy to relate to onscreen.

"We're a group of actors who play a family," he says, describing the show. "Sometimes I'll have a story, then other times the episode will be centered around Alan, Joanna, Tracey, or Jeremy."

Kirk is so dedicated to the show that when he is handed a new script, he reads it carefully and works hard all week at perfecting his acting.

Though many stars treat their first break as a stepping-stone, Kirk says with conviction, "I'm not the kind of guy who gets mad when I don't have that many lines one week. *Growing Pains* is a great show, and it's one of the best experiences I've had so far. I'm just grateful to be part of it."

7. *LIFE OFFSCREEN*

What is Kirk Cameron really like? When he is asked this question, he smiles, blushes, and says, "I'm just a regular guy."

Though many would think Kirk should be egotistical over all the attention he receives, he says matter-of-factly, "It's really no big deal to me. I'm doing everything the same as I always did before all this happened. Actually I feel more fortunate and lucky because I'm getting the chance to do something I really enjoy."

It's clear to see that Kirk is remaining very modest about his career. His overpowering success has not affected him at all. Like any other teenage boy his age, he looks forward to time spent away from the cameras when he can enjoy a day or two all to himself.

"I'm always doing something different," he exclaims. "Whether it's playing soccer, baking muffins, or listening to my stereo, I try to give myself one complete day when I don't have to think about business."

During the first season of *Growing Pains* Kirk

experienced major changes in his life. Before the show brought him public recognition, he had been a pretty casual young man with time to do all the things he liked. But as his popularity grew, time became a very precious thing to Kirk. There just weren't enough hours in the day anymore.

"Lately the only time during the working day that I have to myself is lunch," he reveals. "And sometimes that hour is even taken up because I have to study with the tutor. So I try to take a break somewhere in the middle of the day to collect my thoughts."

With Kirk beginning his reign as the top teen idol, more lines for his character were written into the scripts for *Growing Pains*. Subsequently he found himself working longer hours on the set and having less time for himself.

"I really don't mind it," Kirk comments, "because I love to work. Of course, there are times when I want to go somewhere and do something like play soccer, and I know I can't because I have to work. But I wouldn't trade my career for anything in the world."

Although he's ambitious, Kirk is also a very caring young man.

Kirk knows the value of beginning to practice good health habits at a young age. He is concerned with keeping himself in the best of health and follows the strict Pritikin diet religiously. "A lot of people can't understand why someone so young would be on this diet like I am," he notes. "But I figure, why wait until I'm older to care about my health when I can get an early start now."

At first Kirk was alarmed when reading about the Pritikin diet but was determined to give it a try, anyway. He gave up eating his favorite foods—Mexican and Chinese—as well as eliminating all sugar, butter, and salt. "This diet has a lot to do with the way you will feel in the future," he explains. "It's basically a diet that older people go on. There aren't too many people my age who are interested in it."

The diet is low in protein, sugar, fat, and cholesterol, and high in vegetables, grains, and fruits. It was originally a twenty-eight-day program of diet and exercise, guaranteed safe and healthy by Nathan Pritikin. What Kirk especially likes about it is that, by eating what is allowed, he is able to eat as much as he wants all day.

Though Kirk isn't really concerned with losing weight, he says, "The diet maintains your ideal weight. In other words, you lose so much weight when you go on it and stop losing when you reach the weight you are supposed to be."

The Pritikin diet is not vegetarian; Kirk does eat some meat. However, he prefers muffins for breakfast; and brown rice, a baked potato with no salt or butter, and lots of vegetables for lunch and dinner. Since the diet does not permit any caffeine beverages and forbids coffee and tea, Kirk began limiting what he drinks. Now he likes a bottle of spring water from the French Alps with his meals.

"I'm glad I'm on this diet," he asserts. "Since I started following it over two years ago, I feel much better."

"I think it's important to keep your body physically fit," he says with assurance. "When I'm working on the show, there is always time when I get home to ride my bike or play a game of racquetball. A little exercise keeps your body in shape, and if I didn't find time for it every day, I wouldn't be able to work out with my dad on Saturday. He gets me going with some pretty serious stuff," he adds with a chuckle.

The young superstar cares about his appearance and is dedicated to keeping in shape and staying healthy. Because he is seen across the country on television every Tuesday night, Kirk wouldn't want to look anything but his absolute best. Fortunately he is blessed with natural good looks and is certainly as handsome offscreen as he is on.

His twinkling hazel eyes are a perfect combination of both crystal blue and green. On occasion they even change colors depending on what Kirk wears. "If I wear a blue shirt," he says, "my eyes will look blue. The same thing happens if I wear a deep shade of green. Then they look green."

Since Kirk has been on *Growing Pains* he has grown a full three inches in height. He was five foot six in the first season of the show; now he stands at five foot nine. His weight varies due to his busy schedule. On days when he is rehearsing or filming, he grabs a quick breakfast and lunch. Because he works so hard, Kirk burns up calories very easily. His ideal weight is 130, which he maintains because he is so serious about following the Pritikin diet.

Where does Kirk like to go when he has time off? A California native, he can usually be found sunning himself on the sands of Santa Monica Beach.

In the heat of the summer months Kirk sports a beautiful tan, and since he loves the water so much, some of his favorite activities are water sports. He's an ace swimmer and enjoys waterskiing. "I tried para-sailing once," he admits. "That's where you're sailing in the air and being pulled by a boat. It was really neat, but I don't know if I'll try it again. I think I'll stick to swimming and waterskiing," he asserts, flashing his gorgeous smile.

As a change of pace, Kirk was recently turned on to snow skiing and has learned so fast that he participated in a recent celebrity ski contest in Canada. "I love the feeling of skiing down a slope," he says enthusiastically.

Kirk's favorite day is Saturday, because he is able to catch up on all the things he has no time for all week. He is up at the crack of dawn and heads down to the gym with his dad for a healthy workout session.

When he returns home in early afternoon, he joins his mom in the kitchen and bakes up some of his special muffins and breads from his Pritikin diet recipe book. Kirk's specialties are blueberry muffins and apple-spice cake. "My mother taught me everything I know about baking," he says proudly. "Since she began her own cookie business a few years ago, I got real interested in learning how to bake, and asked her to show me what to do."

Besides baking, Kirk sometimes likes to surprise his family with his own home-cooked meal. "When I have the time, I like to whip up something super for dinner," he says with a twinkle in his eye.

The Camerons' life at home hasn't been disrupted at all by Kirk's stardom. Even though he is the most popular teen idol, starring on both the big screen and small, his life at home remains unchanged. His parents don't treat him any differently, and he's still expected to do his share of work in the house. Kirk's chores for the week are pinned to the refrigerator door along with those of his sisters. Robert and Barbara want their children to be responsible for certain things and don't give them too much leeway. All four children know they must help in the house before going out with friends.

"Dad is real strict," says Kirk. "He'll deduct from my allowance one dollar for every chore we miss." But the young star doesn't mind helping around the house.

"I like keeping my room clean and neat, because I can't stand anything messy," he offers honestly. "When it's my turn, I'll do the dishes and take out the garbage."

When all his work is through, Kirk likes to go out and have a good time. He spends Saturday nights out with his close friends, and though he longs for more freedom, he must be home by a certain hour. "I can't just go anywhere I want," he says. "I have to be in the house by eleven o'clock tops. Sometimes I want to stay out later with some of my friends, but my parents just won't let me."

The one night his parents allowed him to go out and have fun without a curfew was for his first school dance. Though Kirk had to call his parents five times during the night to let them know where he was, it was a perfect evening for the excited ninth-grader.

"I went to the school dance with a group of

friends," he remembers. "First we danced the night away, and then we all chipped in and hired a limousine. We went to a Japanese restaurant for a late dinner, and from there we went to the beach. We stayed for about an hour just taking in the fresh sea air. It was terrific. I had a great time!"

As far as music is concerned, Kirk enjoys going to rock concerts, especially if one of his favorite performers is playing in town. He loves listening to top-40 rock 'n' roll and thinks Prince, Bruce Springsteen, and Billy Joel are the "best singers around today."

When Prince's *Purple Rain* tour played in Los Angeles, Kirk's best friend decided to buy tickets without telling him. The night of the concert, he drove Kirk to the arena and finally told him of his surprise.

"I couldn't believe it," recalls Kirk. "We were sitting in this huge stadium. It was totally dark, and all of a sudden purple lights began flashing all over. It was something I'll never forget."

Another fantastic experience for Kirk was going to Bruce Springsteen's concert. During the first season of *Growing Pains* Alan Thicke treated his co-workers to the Boss's *Born in the U.S.A.* show. "It was very exciting," says Kirk, thinking back to the day he saw Springsteen onstage. "Not only was it the first time I went to one of Bruce's concerts, but I really got to know everyone I worked with."

With his interest in music growing, Kirk decided to take up the piano again. "It's something I always wanted to master," he says. "I try to practice now as much as I can, because I lost a lot of time in between. Sometimes I find I just don't have the time."

In one corner of his bedroom Kirk has an electric piano and a synthesizer system. Whenever he wants to practice, all he has to do is turn everything on and start to play. It's a luxury he wanted to buy when he landed his role as Mike Seaver on *Growing Pains*.

"I really would like to play my keyboards better than I do," he says thoughtfully.

Besides music, Kirk is also a big fan of the movies and likes all kinds of films. "My favorite actor is Eddie Murphy," he comments. "I've seen all his movies, and I think he's *so* funny."

As for Kirk's favorite movie, he confides, "I was real impressed with *Risky Business*. Tom Cruise was great, and I think that the part he played is the ultimate role. I would love to have done it, personally."

His favorite television shows are all comedies. "When I'm home, I never miss *The Cosby Show*, *Cheers*, and *Family Ties*," says Kirk. As for his own show, *Growing Pains*, he smiles. "Oh, it's a favorite, but I'm too critical of myself to watch it."

When Kirk is home on a Tuesday night, he'd much rather go into the quiet of his bedroom and catch up on his homework. When he's finished with that, he likes to turn on his stereo and just relax. "I have everything I need in my bedroom," he explains. "My keyboards, computer, stereo, and all my books."

Kirk likes to read when he has the time. His favorite book is *Catcher in the Rye*, but he finds reading about snakes and spiders to be most interesting. About three years ago Kirk became fascinated with these creatures and began reading everything he could find on them. He soon decided he wanted to have one for a pet and brought home a gopher snake two years ago. Now he has a tarantula spider named Amud, and two snakes; the newest snake is a boa constrictor named Springsteen.

"The only thing you have to do when you have snakes for pets is watch them very carefully," Kirk warns. "They can get away without you knowing about it. Once one of my snakes was lost, and luckily my parents found it in the backyard."

With rare pets, an electric piano, a synthesizer, a stereo, and a home computer all in his bedroom, many would think Kirk is squandering his money on expensive items. That is simply not true. Kirk is a very practical guy who doesn't own anything he doesn't feel he truly needs.

Kirk is careful with his money, and he thinks long before deciding whether or not to buy something extravagant. Being a Libra, Kirk weighs situations before making final decisions.

When he is offscreen, he likes to relax in loose-fitting pants and oversize shirts. He isn't the kind of guy who is serious about the latest fashion for men; he just wears what is comfortable. Although he is concerned about his appearance, Kirk doesn't feel the need to overdress when he's himself, but he is always well dressed. Clothes just seem to fall naturally on Kirk's long, lean physique, and he looks great in everything he wears.

It would seem that since Kirk is the most popular teenager in the country, he should be able to get everything he wants. When he turned sixteen, he was hoping his parents would let him buy a car, but so far Kirk hasn't been able to talk them into it.

Since Barbara drives her son everywhere he needs to go, she doesn't see any reason for him to have his own car. "I'm trying to stall it off as long as possible," she says.

When his parents do agree to his wish to buy his own set of wheels, Kirk knows just the car he wants. "I've dreamed of owning a bright red Porsche 928," he declares with a smile that brings out his gorgeous dimples.

Kirk has described himself as "just a regular guy," and those words ring true to the last syllable. Kirk Cameron is simply spending his teen years as one of Tinseltown's brightest stars. As long as he has time for his family and friends, Kirk is enjoying every minute of the success bestowed on him.

8. *THE GIRL FOR KIRK*

Kirk Cameron is loved by millions of girls who sigh at the mere mention of his name and swoon over his gorgeous face. As the king of teen heartthrobs, he is the most eligible young man in Hollywood, and girls would give anything to catch a glimpse of their favorite guy.

His clean-cut appearance, down-to-earth personality, and undeniable charm excite an entire generation of teenage girls who idolize and dream of him. He enjoys this recognition, but when it comes to the subject of dating, the truth is that Kirk simply has no time.

Though he doesn't lack for a social life, Kirk has said, "Right now it's hard for me to date steady because I'm always working. One day I'm in Los Angeles shooting the show, and the next I'm on a plane to do a press conference in New York. I wouldn't expect a girl to wait for me to come home. I just don't think it would be fair to her."

At seventeen Kirk envisions finding his dream girl to settle down with someday and says he will know immediately when he meets the girl for him.

After all, since he has a good idea of what direction he wants his life to go in, he also knows what traits he is looking for in a girl.

For one thing, her appearance would be very important to Kirk, and he'd like it if she never let too much makeup touch her face. "I like someone who is pretty and doesn't feel the need to pile on heavy makeup," he says. "I also don't think a girl should wear really trendy clothes or have her hair sticking straight up in the air. The girls who dress up like Madonna aren't for me. I much prefer the natural look, someone with just a regular appearance."

Kirk remarks that a girl doesn't have to look like a model to turn his head. More important to him is the way she feels about everything around her. A girl who smiles and likes to have fun is someone Kirk will want to spend more time with.

Kirk is a very loving guy and doesn't let anything stand in the way of displaying his true feelings. His family are the first to agree that when Kirk loves someone, he never lets a day go by without showing his love.

"I grew up in a very affectionate home," he says fondly. "My mom and dad are very close and felt it necessary to raise us the same way."

Because family is so important to Kirk, he would like to bring a girl home for a quiet dinner with the Camerons. He is on the go all day and would enjoy his date coming to his house to spend an evening with him and his family. He has stressed his need for privacy, and staying home is the only way he is truly able to enjoy himself with no interruptions.

As a music lover, Kirk loves to show his dates his piano, synthesizers, and jukeboxes. "We have two fully working jukeboxes in our house." He smiles. "It's really great because we all like different eras of music in my family, and we have records from the fifties and sixties in one jukebox. The other one is dedicated to the music I love. The jukeboxes are real conversational pieces because not too many people own one. When my friends first came over my house, they couldn't believe we actually had *two*."

When Kirk starts playing the music he loves, he can't help but dance to the beat. "I love to dance," he says. "They wrote dancing into an episode of *Growing Pains*, and I really enjoyed doing all those fancy steps," he adds with a twinkle in his eye. Since music and dancing are high on Kirk's list, he loves to take a girl dancing.

"It's important to do things together," says Kirk, thinking ahead. "I think that's one of the secrets of getting along. If you like being together, everything else just comes naturally."

Kirk knows that having someone to confide in through the good times and the bad would be a great comfort to him and his career. The girl for Kirk would understand exactly how important his acting career is to him. She would advise him on what she thinks would be the best moves for his career and would be honest when he asks her opinion on a recent episode of his show. She would realize that acting means everything to him and would care about what makes him happy, just as he would care about what makes her happy.

When he envisions his future, he dreams of marriage, and plans on having his own family someday, just like the happy one he grew up in.

One interviewer asked Kirk the question, "Would you date a fan?" to which he replied a confident, "Sure."

Pondering the idea further, he continued, "My fans are real important to me. I really don't have any objection to dating a fan as long as she is the right girl for me."

Kirk knows he's still too young to think of marriage in the near future and says with a sigh, "Getting married is a big step." At only seventeen years old Kirk has a long way to go before he settles down with one girl.

There are moments, though, when he dreams of someday walking down the magic aisle with someone special to a life of happiness and contentment.

But right now he's dating, meeting different people, and enjoying all that life has to offer.

9. LIKE FATHER, LIKE SON

In January 1987, rumors began circulating around Hollywood concerning a new movie called *Like Father, Like Son*. The producers, Brian Grazer and David Valdes, were beginning to cast their film, and it was no secret that they wanted Kirk for the lead. They had seen his work on *Growing Pains* and were impressed by his talent.

The entertainment news program *Entertainment Tonight*, which had predicted Kirk to be the country's hottest new teen heartthrob, received the news first. Jeanne Wolf announced as part of her "Inside Entertainment" report, "I don't think he even knows it yet, but Kirk Cameron of TV's *Growing Pains* is the producers' choice to play Dudley Moore's son in a new film called *Like Father, Like Son*."

As it turned out, Kirk *didn't* know about it. He was wrapping up the filming for the second season of *Growing Pains* and getting ready to go back to his regular classes in school when he found out.

"I didn't have to audition for this movie," Kirk said later. "The producers just called me up and asked me if I was interested in doing it. They explained the story to me and told me a little about the part, and I asked them to send me the script."

Kirk was very flattered by the way he was approached for *Like Father, Like Son*. It was the first time in his career that he was chosen for a role without having to audition. He was anxious to make another movie and had been offered different parts. Although he didn't accept any of them.

"I was looking for something that would not only be a good movie but also would have a good message," Kirk asserts. "I didn't like any of the scripts I was being sent. *Like Father, Like Son* was a really good script, and I knew after reading it that it would be a good movie to do."

Kirk accepted the role, and instead of joining his classmates in school, he began filming *Like Father, Like Son*. Because the shooting began on March 16 and lasted until May, Kirk had to have a tutor on the set so he could keep up with his schoolwork. Being a junior in high school, he knew he still had one more year to complete his high-school education. He knew how important eleventh grade was and made sure he was on time with all his assignments.

"Next year I plan to go back to school during hiatus so I can graduate with my class," Kirk promised in an interview. "But right now I didn't want to pass up this movie."

Like Father, Like Son was filmed in San Diego and Los Angeles. The principal location for most of Kirk's scenes was John Byrd Junior High School in Sun Valley, California. Although the movie crew was allowed into the school and given freedom to film, classes were in session down the corridor.

Many students wanted to meet Kirk, and during breaks he found himself signing autographs for them.

As the movie began to progress, it became easier for Kirk to adjust to working on his first starring role in a motion picture. In the beginning he found filming a movie difficult because, although he had prior experience on the film *The Best of Times*, his role in that movie had been small.

"I wasn't expected to be on the set all the time like I am now," says Kirk. "I had a few days shooting for *The Best of Times*. But with *Like Father, Like Son*, it took a little time for me to get used to the fact that I have so much to do in this movie."

Like Father, Like Son is a comedy, but above the hilarious comic situations, it has a message that especially appealed to Kirk. The story involves Dr. Jack Hammond (Dudley Moore) and his son Chris, played by Kirk. Chris is constantly confronted by his father over sagging grades at school. His father, a widower raising his son alone, wants Chris to devote more time to school and less time to going out with his best buddy, Trigger (Sean Astin).

A new understanding between Chris and Jack develops thanks to Trigger's uncle Earl, an archaeologist who was given a mysterious potion by a Navajo medicine man for a serious leg injury. While recuperating with Trigger's family, Earl recounts the mystifying short-term mind-switch he experienced after taking the potion. Interested in his story and eager for excitement, Trigger puts some of the potion into an empty Tabasco sauce bottle and brings the bottle to his pal, Chris.

When he gets to Chris's house, Jack and Chris

are arguing and the bottle is accidentally left behind. Father and son use the Tabasco sauce without realizing what it is, and they switch personalities. Now Chris's mind is in Jack's body and vice versa.

Apparently the role reversal couldn't have happened at a worse time and, subsequently, a more humorous time. Jack, a heart surgeon, is expected to be appointed Chief of Staff at one of the world's most high-tech hospitals, and his son has a date with one of the most beautiful and popular girls in school.

The incidents that occur are very funny, but in the end the film tells a strong story of the relationship between father and son. "The father gets a chance to see what it's like to be a teenager today," says Kirk. "He realizes that sometimes it can be tough, and he and his son become closer than they were before."

The script went through numerous changes and rewrites before wrapping up production. When Kirk began working on the movie, he said during an interview, "I read the script only once. Right now it's being changed, I don't have a clear idea of what it's about."

More and more photographers discovered the location of the movie, and followed Kirk everywhere. If they weren't allowed on the set for close shots of him, they snapped Kirk from across the street using zoom lenses.

It was distracting to the cast, but Kirk had learned that this was part of the business he chose to be in. "It really doesn't bother me," he says. "It's just that sometimes you're trying to concentrate on the script and it's difficult to pose for the cameras."

Kirk relished every moment working on the set of *Like Father, Like Son*. He almost couldn't believe the fact that he was starring in a major motion picture and would say after completing the film, "This is a great time for me. Everything is going real well."

10. *LOOKING AHEAD*

What's next for Kirk Cameron? With his ever-growing popularity he is a much-sought-after actor in Hollywood right now. At only seventeen, Kirk has already tackled television and movies successfully, and he knows that acting is something he plans to keep working at.

There is no doubt that he is in demand, and there are many projects being offered to him. So far *Like Father, Like Son* is the only project Kirk has accepted outside of *Growing Pains*, but he plans on doing more films in the future. While he loves being a teen idol, Kirk would someday like to be a serious actor and wants to play a wide variety of roles.

"Naturally I want to do more comedy, because that's what I've had more experience in," he says. "I'm also hoping to do a drama someday."

Kirk has many plans for his future in show business and hopes to write, produce, and direct as well as act. While he dreams of doing other projects, he will never turn his back on *Growing Pains*, the show that gave him his start.

He will always have a very special place in his

heart for the show and says he'll stay with it as long as it is on the air. "*Growing Pains* is very important to me," affirms Kirk. "I'm the type of guy who doesn't turn my back on the people who gave me my first break. I owe them a lot and will never walk out." Then, with a smile, he adds, "Anyway, playing Mike is so much fun."

The role of Mike Seaver has become Kirk Cameron's alter ego. He marvels at the way Mike gets away with certain things and continually wins arguments with his parents. "Mike is real smooth," says Kirk. "He knows exactly what to say to his parents. He always comes up with a quick, witty line when he wants to go out on a school night or when he comes home late. And he often gets away with it. That's something I haven't been able to perfect yet," Kirk adds, reflecting on the fact that his parents keep him under a strict curfew when he goes out with friends.

It's true that Kirk's parents aren't as lenient as Jason and Maggie Seaver, although Kirk does take his character home with him on occasion. "Sometimes I'm saying a line on the show that I want to try with my parents," confides Kirk. "But it never works for me. All my mom says is 'Be Kirk, not Mike.'"

Kirk has no intentions of ever leaving the show. Now that he is breaking into movies and plans to continue working in film, he'll find a way to fit future roles into his *Growing Pains* schedule.

It has already been done successfully by *Family Ties* star Michael J. Fox, and Kirk knows it isn't impossible. When Fox was offered the lead in Steven Spielberg's *Back to the Future*, he worked on his show during the day and filmed the movie at night. This grueling schedule drew attention to the young star whose movies have gone on to win acclaim and break box-office records. Many took notice of Michael, and he is now one of the most popular actors both on television and in the movies.

Kirk is constantly being compared to Michael because of the obvious similarities in their careers. Some reporters have even gone as far as stating that Kirk Cameron *is* the new Michael J. Fox because he is now making his own transition from the small screen to the big. Fortunately these comparisons don't bother Michael or Kirk.

"I could see why people would compare me to Michael," notes Kirk, who has met Fox and liked him. "He started on a hit TV show and has had great success in the movies. Some people are foreseeing that for my future, and I appreciate it. But there really are no similarities between Michael and me. Although I take it as a compliment 'cause I think he's a great actor, I don't go out and try to be just like him. I do my own thing."

Michael surprised Kirk by showing up at the young star's sixteenth birthday party, which was held at the Marriott Hotel in Woodland Hills, California, on October 19, 1986. Barbara threw the party for her famous son, and all his closest friends and family were there to celebrate his turning sixteen.

When Michael walked in unexpectedly, all eyes were on him. Though he didn't follow the suggested dress of wearing black, white, or silver (he wore jeans and a plaid shirt), he walked over to Kirk, wished him a happy birthday, and the two super-stars sat at a table discussing their careers.

"Michael has his whole career in perspective," Kirk said of him after they met. "He told me not to take anything seriously and to have fun with everything that came my way. And I said, 'Michael, that's just what I'm doing.' If all this ended tomorrow, I would probably go through with my first ambition to become a doctor. I was always good in science, and I figure it's good to be interested in something else just in case acting doesn't work out."

As a young boy, Kirk dreamed of studying medicine and becoming a doctor one day. He has said in numerous interviews that he still plans to go through with his original dream if his career begins to slip. "I'm realistic," he states. "I know that someday acting might not be there for me."

What about his immediate future? He is now a senior in high school and is beginning to think seriously of what he wants to do when he graduates.

"I plan on going to college," he announces. "But I don't think I'll be going to medical school right now. There is so much happening with my career that I want to concentrate on acting."

He is the hottest actor in Hollywood right now and is enjoying every minute of his enormous popularity. He realizes that success like his could be fleeting and that one morning he could wake up to find all his fame gone. After all, his popularity happened so fast. He went from being an unknown child actor to one of the best-known young actors in the country in a short time.

When Kirk is asked what he'd like to be doing in

five years, he shies away from answering. There is no way he could possibly imagine what his future will hold, so he doesn't think about it.

"I don't have any plans," he says. "I would like to stay in show business and maybe write and direct someday, but right now I'm so busy, I really don't have the time to think about tomorrow. I'm just taking one day at a time."

Kirk Cameron is a talented young man with a bright future who is proving to be the most exciting screen presence of the 1980s. "I have a lot I want to do," he says self-confidently. "I just hope the job offers keep coming in."

For Kirk Cameron, the top teen heartthrob in the country today, the next job is just around the corner.

KIRK'S VITAL STATISTICS

Full Real Name: Kirk Thomas Cameron
Birthdate: October 12, 1970
Birthplace: Panorama City, California
Astrological Sign: Libra
Height: 5'9"
Weight: 130 lbs.
Eyes: Hazel
Hair: Light brown
Family: Parents, Robert and Barbara; three younger sisters, Bridgette, Melissa, and Candace
First Acting Break: Super Sugar Crisp television commercial at age 9
Television: *Two Marriages* and *Growing Pains;* guest appearances on *Bret Maverick, Lou Grant,* and *Code Red*
TV Movies: *Goliath Awaits; Children of the Crossfire; Starflight One; The Woman Who Willed a Miracle; Andrea's Story, A Hitchhiking Tragedy; Beyond Witch Mountain*
Films: *The Best of Times* with Kurt Russell, Robin Williams and Tracey Gold; *Like Father, Like Son* with Dudley Moore and Sean Astin

FAVORITES:
Sports: Racquetball, soccer, tennis, skiing
Movie: *Risky Business*
TV Shows: *The Cosby Show, Cheers, Family Ties*
Actor: Eddie Murphy
Actress: JoBeth Williams
Music: Top-40
Song: "Raspberry Beret" by Prince
Singers: Prince, Bruce Springsteen, Billy Joel
Bands: INXS, Tears for Fears
Clothes: Jeans and T-shirts, oversize pants and big shirts
Food: Pritikin muffins (he bakes them himself)
Dessert: Apple-spice cake
Car: Red Porsche 928
Book: *Catcher in the Rye*
School Subject: Science
Game: Trivial Pursuit
Place: The beach
Instruments Played: Piano and synthesizer
Most Prized Possessions: "My synthesizer and jukeboxes!"
Pets: Two snakes and a tarantula spider named Amud
Best Friends: Jason Bateman, Ricky Schroder
Places He Would Like to Visit: Switzerland, Ireland, Paris
Where to Meet Kirk: Santa Monica Beach
Where to Write to Kirk: Kirk Cameron
                                           c/o *Growing Pains*
                                           Warner Brothers
                                               Television
                                           4000 Warner Blvd.
                                           Burbank, CA 91522

KIRK TRIVIA

Kirk has snakes and a spider for pets because he is allergic to cat and dog hair.

Three goals Kirk has set for himself are to be the best actor possible, to eat nutritious foods, and to get good grades in school.

Kirk likes to ski at Lake Tahoe and Mountain High.

He thinks model Christie Brinkley is "very pretty," and he'd like to meet her someday.

Kirk's favorite color is green.

Kirk loves to water-ski and says, "One day I'm going to try it barefoot."

Kirk receives over two thousand fan letters a day.

Kirk has no regrets about having started so young in acting. "I know some kids who started even younger," he says. "It's been a lot of fun, and it's getting better all the time."

Kirk has never seen any of Woody Allen's, Laurence Olivier's, or Marlon Brando's movies.

The first time Kirk ever saw an R-rated movie was when his dad rented *Risky Business* starring Tom Cruise.

Kirk works nine hours a day, five days a week, on *Growing Pains*.

Kirk loves to talk on the phone. Three years ago his parents gave him a phone for Christmas.

Kirk does his homework on a home computer in his bedroom.

Kirk is a science-fiction fan.

Kirk loves going to the top of Chatsworth Hills to look at the beautiful view of the San Fernando Valley.

Kirk has never tasted chocolate.

Kirk's sister Candace appeared in the John Hughes film, *Some Kind of Wonderful*, and is one of the stars of the new show, *Full House*, with John Stamos.

The Cameron family can trace their ancestors back to the Civil War.

Kirk lives with his family in a big, ranch-style house in Canoga Park, California. "It's a little old-fashioned, but my room is pretty modern," he says.

Kirk's favorite game is Trivial Pursuit. His favorite category is Science and Nature.

KIRK'S WORDS
OF WISDOM

On Acting
"The best part of acting is the challenge. To see if you can really pull it off and have people believe you're someone else."

"Most kids don't get to experience TV stuff. They see it, but it's sort of an unimaginable world to them. And I'm behind it all."

On Actors He'd Like to Work With
"I've been friends with Jason Bateman since we were little. We were on the same soccer team and I've always said someday I want to do a movie with him and Rick Schroder."

On Success
"I never expected it to happen. When I first started on the show, people at school were asking me to sign their yearbooks, and I had never even met them before."

"Some stars take success too seriously. I feel very fortunate to have so much."

On Fans

"I sometimes hear about girls who have crushes on me, but unfortunately I don't get the chance to meet most of them."

"I like people who appreciate my work and let me know it."

On His Family

"I am very close to my parents and sisters. The time I spend with them is very important to me. My mom has really done a lot for me, and I'm grateful. Without the support of my family, I don't think I would have stayed in acting."

On School

"I take my education very seriously. It's important for me to keep my grades up because I'm planning on going to college."

On the Pritikin Diet

"In the beginning, when I first started reading about it, I got scared. I thought, 'Why am I doing this?' But I'm glad I went on it because now I feel so much better. I have a lot more energy."

On His Character, Mike Seaver

"Mike is just like any other teenager. He likes to hang around with his friends, dance, and go to parties. He's a little bit too confident sometimes, but he has a great sense of humor and loves to have a good time."

On Girls
"I like girls who look natural and are down-to-earth. I wouldn't want a girl to like me just because I'm on TV."

On Dating
"The truth is, I work so much that it's hard for me to date right now. I just don't have the time."

On Watching Himself on Television
"I was excited to see myself acting on TV the first time, but I've never been completely satisfied with my performance. Even as far back as the first commercial I was in, I saw things I wanted to change the next time. I used to watch myself on *Growing Pains*, but now I never turn it on. I'm much too critical of myself."

On His Character, Chris Hammond, in Like Father, Like Son
"My character is similar to Mike Seaver. Chris is a teenager just trying to be cool, and his dad is a heart surgeon who doesn't understand him. It's as if Chris isn't good enough for his dad. He never quite measures up to his dad's expectations."

On His Future
"I want to stay in acting. Maybe someday I'll write, direct, and produce."

ABOUT THE AUTHOR

GRACE CATALANO is the editor of the popular teen magazine, *Dream Guys*. She has interviewed scores of celebrities and her articles have appeared in numerous movie magazines. To commemorate the tenth anniversary of the death of Elvis Presley, she and her brother, Joseph, wrote and designed *Elvis—A 10th Anniversary Tribute*. Grace lives with her family in Valley Stream, New York.